First Steps in the SAP® Production Processes (PP)

Second Edition

Björn Weber

Thank you for purchasing this book from Espresso Tutorials!

Like a cup of espresso coffee, Espresso Tutorials SAP books are concise and effective. We know that your time is valuable and we deliver information in a succinct and straightforward manner. It only takes our readers a short amount of time to consume SAP concepts. Our books are well recognized in the industry for leveraging tutorial-style instruction and videos to show you step by step how to successfully work with SAP.

Check out our YouTube channel to watch our videos at
https://www.youtube.com/user/EspressoTutorials.

If you are interested in SAP Finance and Controlling, join us at
http://www.fico-forum.com/forum2/
to get your SAP questions answered and contribute to discussions.

Related titles from Espresso Tutorials:

▶ Tanya Duncan: Practical Guide to SAP® CO-PC (Product Cost Controlling) *http://5064.espresso-tutorials.com*

▶ Uwe Göhring: Capacity Planning with SAP®
http://5080.espresso-tutorials.com

▶ Avijt Dutta & Shreekant Shiralkar: Demand Planning with SAP® APO—Concepts and Design
http://5105.espresso-tutorials.com

▶ Avijt Dutta & Shreekant Shiralkar: Demand Planning with SAP® APO—Execution
http://5106.espresso-tutorials.com

▶ Rosana Fonseca: Practical Guide to SAP® Material Ledger (ML)
http://5116.espresso-tutorials.com

▶ Tobias Götz, Anette Götz: Practical Guide to SAP® Transportation Management (2nd edition) *http://5082.espresso-tutorials.com*

▶ Claudia Jost: First Steps in the SAP® Purchasing Processes (MM), Second Edition *http://5166.espresso-tutorials.com*

▶ Matthew Johnson: SAP® Material Master—A Practical Guide, 2nd extended version
http://5190.espresso-tutorials.com

Björn Weber
First Steps in the SAP® Production Processes (PP), Second Edition

ISBN:	978-1-71947-100-8
Editor:	Anja Achilles
Translation:	Tracey Duffey
Cover Design:	Philip Esch
Cover Photo:	© Herrndorff, # 74074507 – stock.adobe.com
Interior Book Design:	Johann-Christian Hanke

Feedback
We greatly appreciate any kind of feedback you have concerning this book. Please mail us at *info@espresso-tutorials.com*.

Table of Contents

Foreword

Dear reader,

You have decided to take a look at a tutorial about production planning in SAP ERP. This suggests two things: firstly, that you (probably) have no desire to wade through long, excessive books on SAP standard software; secondly, that you are interested in production planning, either for your studies or due to your work, and wish to find out how it is implemented in SAP ERP.

In recent decades, production planning, just like all industrial production, has undergone a fundamental change. Whilst the period of economic boom was marked by long delivery times and a limited product selection, known as a "sellers' market," today there is an unlimited quantity of different offers with quick availability of just a few days, even for customer-specific products. Today, the "buyers' market" prevails.

Production planning has had to (and still has to!) adapt to these changing circumstances. Previously, the correct calculation of the required quantity of components (MRP: Material Requirements Planning), and the greatest possible utilization of production resources were important for planning, but today, the requirements are much higher. Naturally, the aim is still to use resources to the best possible advantage. At the same time, however, production—and thus also planning—must be highly flexible to enable customer wishes to be implemented at short notice. These contradictory objectives are linked to the expectation of high planning reliability—i.e., delivery reliability. Planning is therefore becoming increasingly complex and usually cannot be done without software support. This is where the PP (Production Planning) module of SAP ERP and other planning programs come into play. You can use these programs to generate master production schedules that meet the specified framework conditions and objectives and to monitor the implementation of these schedules.

This book presents the basics of production planning in SAP ERP. In Chapter 1, I present the planning concepts that form the basis for the PP module and outline an example that is the basis for the process descriptions in subsequent chapters. I not only look at Manufacturing Resource Planning (MRP II), but also at the planning-driven classification of products based on the order penetration point, explaining the production approaches engineer-to-order, make-to-order, assemble-to-order, and make-to-stock.

Building on this, Chapter 2 explains how, in the design and work scheduling phase, the master data required for planning is created in SAP ERP. This chapter also explains the importance of this data for production planning and control. In Chapter 3, I show you how to forecast sales figures in SAP ERP and, based on these figures, create a production program. In Chapter 4, based on these explanations, you will learn how quantity demand planning works and how it is implemented. You will learn how the defined master data influences the planning and how you can analyze the results yourself. Chapter 5 presents Shop Floor Control and the production orders it uses. You will learn how these elements are structured and what steps they undergo during the course of production. Finally, in Chapter 6, I show you how to perform capacity leveling in an SAP system.

My intention with this book is to offer a clear introduction to the planning processes with SAP ERP and to help you to more easily complete the tasks assigned to you. However, you should also look beyond the procedure described here and try out other functions to make processes even more effective. There is always more than one way to do something.

Acknowledgments

This book is dedicated to anyone who looks at the world with open eyes and is always ready for change.

Many thanks to my wife and proofreader for her patience and understanding during the writing of this book, enabling me to focus on the essentials of the manuscript even in times of stress.

At this point, I would also like to thank Jörg Siebert and Martin Munzel for their extraordinary vision of packaging important SAP content into e-books that do not have to be weighty tomes.

I hope that this book also enables many users who otherwise often take a step back when presented with extensive technical books to look at the wide and varied options provided by this software. The aim of this book is to enable these users and you, dear reader, to have the confidence to look beyond the boundaries of the well-traveled paths and to critically ask: can we improve what we have always done—perhaps since we introduced SAP in our company—even further? I hope that, with this book, I can help you to make these improvements.

We have added a few icons to highlight important information. These include:

Tips	
	Tips highlight information that provides more details about the subject being described and/or additional background information.

Examples	
	Examples help illustrate a topic better by relating it to real world scenarios.

Videos	
	Go to the homepage of Espresso Tutorials to watch a video.

Attention	
	Attention notices highlight information that you should be aware of when you go through the examples in this book on your own.

Finally, a note concerning the copyright: all screenshots printed in this book are the copyright of SAP SE. All rights are reserved by SAP SE. Copyright pertains to all SAP images in this publication. For the sake of simplicity, we do not mention this specifically underneath every screen-shot.

1 Production planning

"The wise man must be wise before,
not after, the event."

(Epicharmus, approx. 550 BC–460 BC)

In this chapter, I present the basic planning approaches used in the SAP system. I also present the most important planning strategies and outline the example used in subsequent chapters.

1.1 Planning approaches

MRP II (*manufacturing resource planning*) is a planning concept that is a further development of material requirements planning (MRP). In this concept, based on quantity calculation, previous and subsequent planning steps have been defined to enable integrated production planning.

Thus, sales and operations planning and demand program planning for defining primary requirements quantities (known as "independent requirements") have been placed before material requirements planning, while scheduling with consideration of limited capacities for detailed planning has been added after MRP. The diagram in Figure 1.1 shows all phases of the MRP II concept which I will address in more detail below.

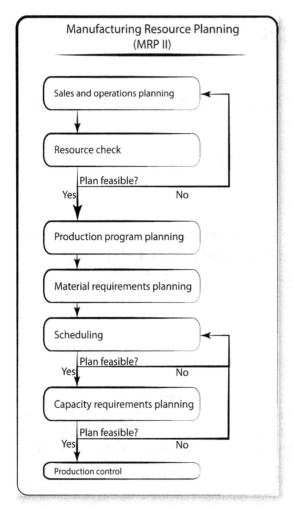

Figure 1.1: Planning phases of the MRP II concept

Sales planning involves itemizing the quantity of planned sales of products and spare parts. It can take place at an aggregated level or can be based on individual materials. Product groups, customers, and geographical regions are examples of possible aggregation levels. With regard to time, the requirements can be shown in weeks, months, or quarters. During *operations planning*, production quantities are created for the determined sales figures. To ensure that the planning is as accurate as possible, coverage ranges or production intervals can be considered. Rough-cut planning profiles can be used to create loads to estimate the planning feasibility. These profiles reflect the resource requirements at aggregated level and, in conjunction with the available capacity of the corresponding resources, enable an initial analysis of feasibility. The results of this analysis can lead to sales targets being reviewed with the sales department or can provide the incentive for planning investments to increase capacities.

The requirement figures that have been subject to this plausibility check are then handed over to the demand management organization. Here, the requirements, which were previously available at aggregated level (based on time and hierarchy), are broken down. You do not have to distribute the requirements evenly; for example, you can use a distribution based on past consumption. The *planned independent requirements* now available at material level are offset against any existing specific sales orders. The *planning strategy* defined for this material also determines how this comparison is performed and in what period (see Section 1.2).

From the independent, planned, and customer requirements, material requirements planning determines the quantities of assemblies, components, standard parts, and raw materials required. To enable this, *production batches* are created. These planning elements have a finish date, a lead time, and a bill of material. These values are used to calculate the dates for which the quantities are required. These requirements are compared with existing stocks and any expected stock receipts in order to calculate any material quantity that needs to be procured. If, during lead time scheduling, receipt elements are created and the requirements for these elements cannot be covered in time, this is documented and the MRP controller can check, for example, whether the lead time can be reduced. If this is not possible, the controller can initiate an adjustment of the independent requirements to the determined bottleneck. This ensures that the second feasibility check level is implemented here.

Before the production department starts to implement the planning, the MRP controller can plan capacity requirements. To do so, they compare the capacity requirements created at the resources with the available capacity. If the result shows a capacity overload situation, they can use a planning table to perform specific sequencing against the limited capacity available and thus resolve the overload. Receipt dates for components may slip beyond the requirements date. In this case, the quantity planning may have to be repeated.

Shop Floor Control monitors and corrects production execution. This includes creating and releasing production orders, printing production documents, and reporting production progress. This last activity is particularly relevant for the MRP controllers, as they use the reports to determine whether production is progressing according to plan or whether an adjustment is required.

As you can see, the MRP II concept is divided into phases that include internal check loops but that are connected only by an aligned forwarding of values. When IT systems were first developed, and processor performance and storage were seriously restricted, this structure had the significant advantage that every phase could be considered and modeled in isolation. Thus, limited complexity enabled the programming of systems that could calculate solutions within a finite time. As a result, the MRP II concept established itself in most corporate programs.

Today, scholars involved with the topic and software companies (with their products) try to link quantity planning and capacity requirements planning. They use various approaches to do this:

- ▶ Heuristics
- ▶ Linear optimization
- ▶ Complex planning tables

However, there are also further developments for simplifying planning activities in the upstream sales and operations planning processes:

- ▶ Fewer aggregation levels
- ▶ Consideration of logistical capacities
- ▶ Detailed requirements profiles

1.2 Planning strategies

A decisive criterion for planning is the *order penetration point*. On one hand, this describes the step in the value-added chain from which the sales order "pulls" the procurement; i.e., the point at which the customer for whom something is being produced is clear. On the other hand, it defines the step by which the procurement is "pushed" from preliminary planning or forecasting; i.e., is only produced anonymously (see Figure 1.2).

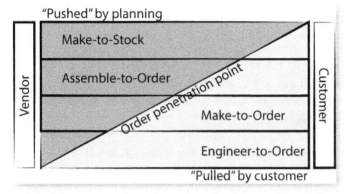

Figure 1.2: Planning strategies and order penetration point

Make-to-stock is the simplest planning strategy. Here, a product is procured and produced, including all components, based only on preliminary planning up to the point that it arrives in the shipping warehouse. This strategy enables good alignment of the production of all components, as well as high utilization of production resources. It also guarantees the shortest delivery times of all strategies. However, in contrast to these advantages, there is a risk of over-production and results in excess stock. Short planning can also be problematic, because it (often) restricts the production flexibility. Any impending deficit is difficult to prevent, and thus the expected delivery time can be difficult to achieve or cannot be achieved at all.

The *assemble-to-order* strategy can, to some extent, be used to alleviate the risk of excess stock. With this strategy, only the components are procured or produced, based on planning. They are then only assembled to create a finished product when a sales order is received. The level of the desired lower stocks depends to a large extent on the proportion of value added by the assembly. Also, the greater the number of variants for a product, the greater the benefits of this strategy, because less value is connected to the less frequently required variants. The prerequisite for successful implementation of this strategy is flexible assembly that enables customer requirements to be implemented with regard to delivery time.

15

Make-to-order is an approach in which products designed and prepared for production are only produced on customer request. As the company generally only stores the raw materials, the delivery time using this strategy is considerably longer than the approaches above. However, to enable a short delivery time as required by the customer, the machines, and the employees, must be flexible; i.e., available on demand. One advantage of this strategy is that the stock risk is minimized.

Finally, *engineer-to-order* describes a concept where customers request products that have not yet been designed when the order is placed and that have to be produced individually. This strategy has the longest delivery time of all the approaches presented, and results in a further planning problem: because an ordered product has not yet been precisely defined, it is particularly difficult to accurately plan the delivery date.

Empirical values from similar products are usually used to help determine the delivery time. But what about the components? They can only be procured once the design has been completed; for example, the risk could be too high that this time special steel is needed instead of standard steel. This special material, or the exceptional purchased part, represents the greatest risk for not meeting the deadline. If the materials required are not clear until after the design, it is sometimes too late to order the materials for punctual delivery. See Table 1.1.

	Replenishment lead time	Stock risk	Production flexibility
Make-to-stock	Not applicable	High	Low
Assemble-to-order	Low	Low	Medium
Make-to-order	High	Not applicable	High
Engineer-to-order	Very high	Not applicable	High

Table 1.1: Advantages and disadvantages of production strategies

1.3　Definition of the example

During the course of this book, I use an example to illustrate the individual production planning processes in the SAP system. To help you to better understand the illustrations from the individual transactions, I will first briefly present the example product used.

In this book, our example product is a bicycle, so we are looking at a bicycle manufacturing company. Production is according to a make-to-stock strategy (see Section 1.2). This means that for this salable product, planned independent requirements that reflect the expected sales are available from the sales department. As some of the parts of the bicycle in our example have to be designed from the very beginning, not all master data will have been created by the beginning of the planning. Therefore, before production planning can take place, we have to create the master data.

The bicycle in our example has the material designation ET-F-WT500. It consists of a complete (CP) frame (ET-1010), produced in-house, a front wheel (ET-1005) and a rear wheel (ET-1006), two pedals (ET-1007), the chain (ET-1013), and the complete (CP) gears (ET-1014). The components mentioned are all purchased from other suppliers (with the exception of the frame). The complete bicycle frame assembly consists of the frame (ET-1011), the fork (ET-1012), the saddle (ET-1003), and the handlebars (ET-1004). Figure 1.3 shows the composition. The new parts developed are:

► ET-F-WT500—bicycle WT500

► ET-1014—gears CP

► ET-1011—frame

► ET-1010—bicycle frame CP

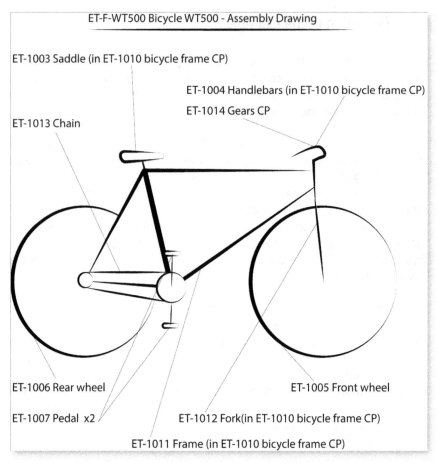

Figure 1.3: Illustration of the example product

SAP ERP recognizes various organizational elements, of which *plant* is the decisive element for production and production planning. All processes for our example take place in plant 1200. All further relevant master data and definitions are covered in the following chapters.

2 Design and work scheduling

During the design and work scheduling phase, you define the master data required for subsequent production planning and control.

In this chapter, I explain in detail the master data required for planning, and the importance of this data. Firstly, I outline the material master and bill of material (the design data) to create the basis for explaining the work center and routing (the production data).

2.1 Material master

In our example (see Section 1.3), we designed a new bicycle and the design department will now provide a more detailed design. This includes creating the material master data and all new components for the product in SAP ERP to enable entry of further master data.

The material master contains basic information to describe the material, as well as parameters for controlling the company processes. It consists of several views that group values into their areas of application (design, sales and distribution, production, etc.). Some views are valid across the group of companies, while others relate to specific organizational units; for example, a plant or a purchasing organization. The sales and distribution view contains data that is important for the sales and distribution process, such as discount groups. These details are only valid for the corresponding sales organization. The accounting view contains valuation classes for correctly classifying the material for book-keeping, for example, and these valuation classes are valid only for the corresponding company code. Four views are interesting for production planning:

▶ Basic data view (across the group)

▶ MRP view (plant-specific)

▶ Work scheduling view (plant-specific)

▶ Forecasting view (plant-specific)

Initially, the designer is only able to create the basic data view. The remaining views are created and filled during the course of work scheduling. The BASIC DATA 1 view contains basic information about the materials (see Figure 2.1). In addition to the material number and the material text, this information includes:

▶ the base unit of measure ❶,

▶ identification code for the design group responsible ❷,

▶ information about the weight ❸,

▶ information about the size/dimensions ❹,

▶ and much more.

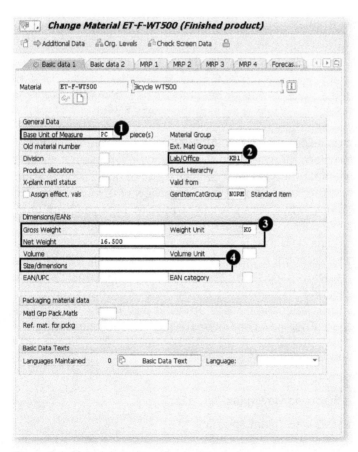

Figure 2.1: Material master—Basic data 1 view

For our example, the designer now creates the material masters for the complete bicycle *ET-F-WT500*, the new frame, the new gears, and the new component "complete bicycle frame". To do this, in SAP ERP, transaction MM01 is called up: SAP MENU • LOGISTICS • PRODUCTION • MASTER DATA • MATERIAL MASTER • MATERIAL • CREATE (GENERAL). The following initial screen appears (see Figure 2.2):

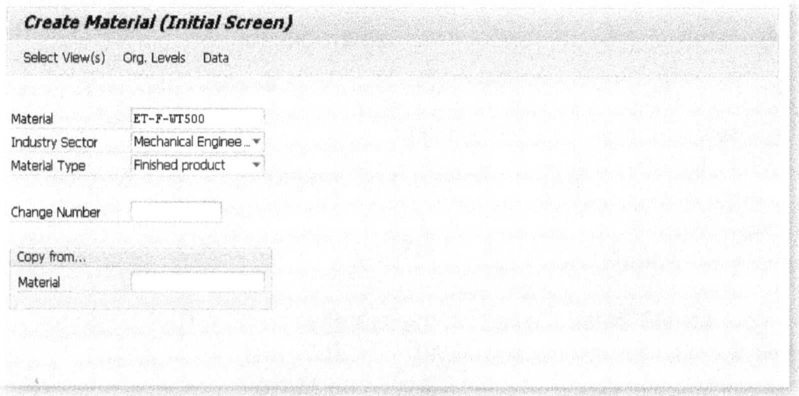

Create Material (Initial Screen)

Select View(s)   Org. Levels   Data

Material	ET-F-WT500
Industry Sector	Mechanical Enginee... ▾
Material Type	Finished product ▾

Change Number

Copy from...
Material

Figure 2.2: Creating a material (initial screen)

The designer enters the material for the finished bicycle (*ET-F-WT500*) and selects the industry sector for the bicycle (*Mechanical Engineering*), and the material type (*Finished Product*).

Next, this information is confirmed by pressing ⌷Enter⌷, the first basic data view opens again (see Figure 2.1. Here, the engineering group *KB1* is selected in the LAB/OFFICE field ❷; *PC* (for "piece") is entered in the BASE UNIT OF MEASURE field ❶ and in the NET WEIGHT ❸ and DIMENSIONS ❹ fields, and the values from the design documentation are adopted. On the BASIC DATA 2 tab, the material is entered (e.g., *Aluminum*) for the frame, and references to the already-stored design documentation are created.

All other components in our example are transferred from existing bicycles and therefore do not need to be created. The designer can only create the *bill of material* when all the material masters have been created in the SAP system.

The remaining three views are either created now and filled with standard values that are to be made more specific later, or are set up entirely at a later time by the work schedulers or responsible MRP controllers. However, I will present them briefly here.

The MRP VIEW offers four tabs on which you can set all parameters for procuring the material. The values it contains define the production planning and control for the article. Here, for example, you enter settings for the following criteria:

▶ external procurement or in-house production,

▶ planning-driven or consumption-driven materials planning,

▶ size of the procurement batch,

▶ individual customer production or anonymous make-to-stock production,

▶ safety stock, etc.

Let's now create these views for the material ET-F-WT500 together. To do this, we call up transaction MM01 via: SAP MENU • LOGISTICS • PRODUCTION • MASTER DATA • MATERIAL MASTER • MATERIAL • CREATE GENERAL MATERIAL, and enter the material number. Because the basic data for this material has already been created, the SAP ERP system adds the data for the industry sector and material type. In the dialog box that appears, we select the views *MRP 1, MRP 2, MRP 3, MRP 4*, and *Work Scheduling* by clicking the relevant button to the left of the designation. After clicking the green checkmark ✅ to confirm our selection, in the next dialog box we select plant *1200,* and confirm again.

MRP profiles

MRP profiles enable users to group the settings for the *MRP view* and save them as default values. When a new material is created, the fields defined in the profile are then filled with the default values. This simplifies the process of creating and maintaining materials.

The transactions for maintaining the MRP profiles can be found under: SAP MENU • LOGISTICS • PRODUCTION • MASTER DATA • MATERIAL MASTER • PROFILE • MRP PROFILE.

When creating the MRP view, you then select the profile in the ORGANIZATIONAL LEVELS dialog box (see Figure 2.3).

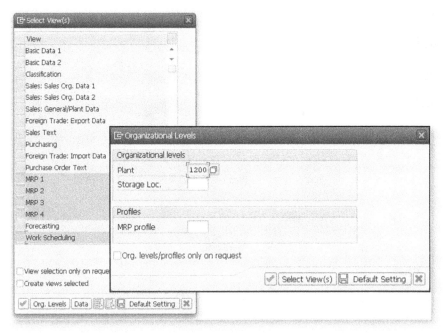

Figure 2.3: View selection and organizational levels

The first tab that we see now is MRP 1 (Figure 2.4). In addition to the GENERAL DATA area, the tab contains the areas MRP PROCEDURE and LOT SIZE DATA, where you can define parameters.

MRP TYPE is a mandatory field; because we receive planned require-ment quantities for the finished product, the material should be planned on a consumption basis. Therefore, we select *PD* here. In the MRP CON-TROLLER field, to ensure that the controller responsible can subsequently analyze the planning, we enter the relevant key, here *000*. The procure-ment proposal should always cover one week, and we therefore select *WB* in the LOT SIZE field. We do not need any further settings for the lot size data for our product.

When we confirm with ⌞Enter⌟, the SAP ERP system checks whether we have entered information in all mandatory fields and, if so, jumps to the next tab. If entries are missing from mandatory fields, a warning mes-sage or error message appears in the lower part of the SAP system win-dow.

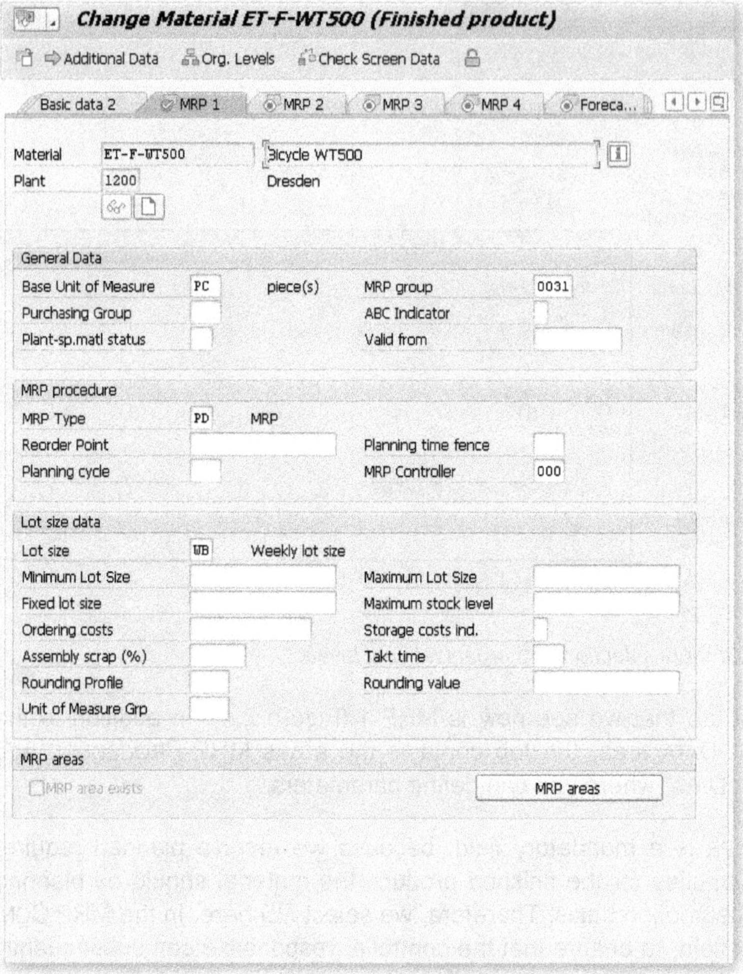

Figure 2.4: Material master tab—MRP 1 view

On the MRP 2 tab (see Figure 2.5), we see values in the PROCUREMENT, SCHEDULING, and NET REQUIREMENTS CALCULATION areas.

Because we want to assemble the bicycle exclusively ourselves, in the PROCUREMENT TYPE field we select *E* (the value for "own production"). We also enter a value in the PRODUCTION STORAGE LOCATION field—the storage location from which the components are removed and to which the finished product is delivered (here: *0002*).

Because we manufacture the material ourselves, we have to enter a value in the IN-HOUSE PRODUCTION field; here, we select 2 days because the average weekly production time for a bicycle of the type in our example is two days. In the GR PROCESSING TIME field, we select 1 day. This indicates that the stock is not available until the second day after the end of the order. There can be various reasons for this time buffer in the actual process flow; for example, there is a quarantine period until all quality results are available, or time is required for the shipping packaging to be attached. In the SCHEDULING MARGIN KEY field, we enter 000; this determines the different scheduling buffers described in more detail in Section 5.2.

Because no safety stocks are planned for this material, no entries are necessary here.

Figure 2.5: Material master tab—MRP 2 view

On the MRP 3 tab (see Figure 2.7), we define some settings relating to the *preliminary planning behavior*. In the STRATEGY GROUP field, we select *40 (Planning with final assembly)*.

The strategy group controls the behavior of independent requirements—both customer requirements and planned requirements—as well as how they are included in the requirements planning. With the strategy "Planning with final assembly", both customer requirement quantities and planned requirement quantities are considered in the requirements planning. However, with this strategy, requirements planning attempts to offset the two requirements against one another because the planned requirement quantities are merely an expression of an expected customer order. This behavior is controlled with the *consumption mode* and *consumption periods*. The consumption mode defines the temporal direction, starting from the customer order, in which the system searches for planned independent requirements for consumption. The consumption periods specify the number of days, starting from the customer order, that the system should search in the past or in the future (see Figure 2.6)

Figure 2.6: Consumption of planned requirement

The bicycle in our example should receive weekly planned independent requirements—they are always imported into the SAP ERP system on Mondays. To ensure that customer orders that are to be delivered during the week are offset only against the planned independent requirements of that week, we enter *1* (Backward consumption only) in the CONSUMPTION MODE field, and in the BACKWARD CONSUMPTION PERIOD field, we enter a value of *5* days. This means that for every customer order, the system searches backwards five days for planned requirement quantities that the customer order quantity can be offset against (see Section 4.1).

In the AVAILABILITY CHECK field, we select *01*. This parameter controls how the *ATP check* (see Section 5.3) is applied to this material. For the finished product, this check is performed from a customer order, and for a component, from an assembly order; the setting 01 is sufficient in our example.

The precise effects of the different settings in the AVAILABILITY CHECK field depend on your system settings. Section 5.3 looks at the availability check for an assembly order.

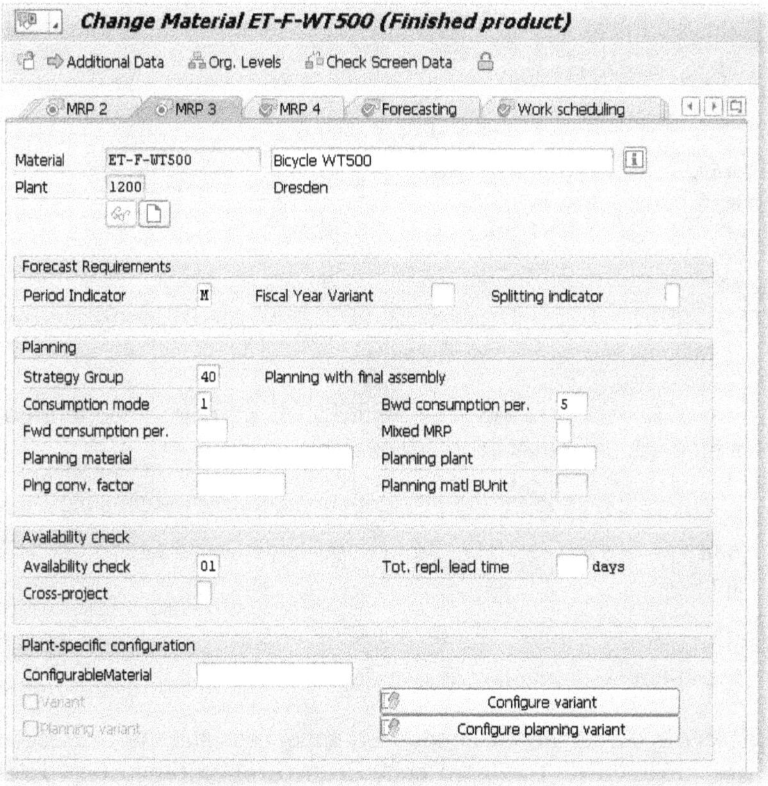

Figure 2.7: Material master tab—MRP 3 view

On the MRP 4 tab (see Figure 2.8), we do not have to enter any information for our example because the BOM explosion and the selection of production versions are not relevant.

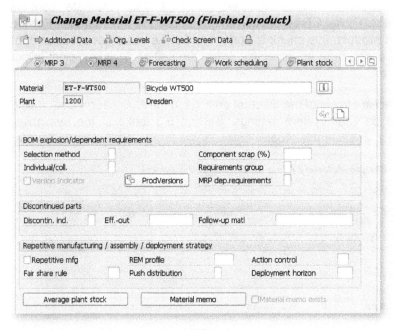

Figure 2.8: Material master tab—MRP 4 view

On the WORK SCHEDULING tab (see Figure 2.9), we enter important parameters for production execution; for example:

▶ identification code for the production supervisor responsible,

▶ storage location to which the material is delivered after production,

▶ batch or serialization obligation, and

▶ the in-house production time in days.

For our bicycle, we define the production supervisor and the production scheduling profile here. The latter entry controls which production order type the system proposes for this material. This saves time again later when these orders are created (see Chapter 5).

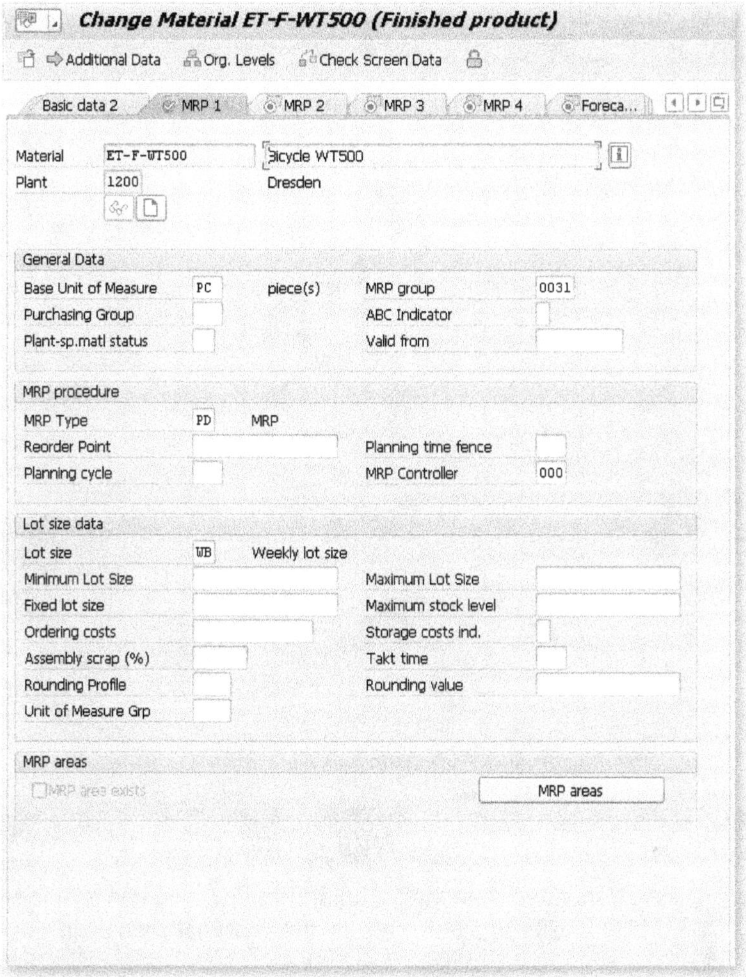

Figure 2.9: Material master tab—Work scheduling view

Figure 2.10 shows the FORECASTING tab that contains all the data re-quired for performing a material forecast and that forms the basis for consumption-driven materials planning. The most important parameters relate to:

► Forecast model

► Past periods

► Forecast interval

Figure 2.10: Material master tab—Forecasting view

Creating material master views for production planning

A short video demonstration shows how you can add the MRP and production data to the material master in the PP module in practice: see
https://espresso-tutorials.com/PP.php

Recommended reading

In his book "The SAP Material Master—a Practical Guide", Matthew Johnson explains in great detail how to set up and handle the material master in an SAP system. This book was published by Espresso Tutorials in 2013.

2.2   Bill of material

In SAP ERP, a *bill of material* (BOM) is a structured collection of elements. As these elements can be very different, SAP recognizes various categories of bill of material. It is not the type of presentation that determines the differentiation, but the content or use of the list. In the SAP system, the following BOM categories are available:

▶ Material BOM

▶ Document structure

▶ Order BOM

▶ Project BOM

A *material BOM* describes the structure of a material made from individual components or other assemblies, and represents the most frequently used category of BOM. A *document structure* structures complex documents. For example, the documentation for a system can consist of a manual with electrical and hydraulic circuit diagrams, as well as technical drawings that have all been stored individually. *Order BOMs* and *project BOMs* are usually lists of materials that are valid only for a specific order or project respectively. They can be used to record special features (e.g., customer-specific adjustments to the product) without changing the fundamental BOM.

A bill of material consists of the header and one or more items. The former contains basic information, such as the base quantity of the bill of material or the engineering group (laboratory/office) responsible, as well as a description of the alternative BOM and its status (active or inactive).

Every BOM item contains exactly one component. The quantity and item category (e.g., stock item or text item) of the component required to create the base quantity are also stored here, as well as other control parameters required for special applications.

You can find these control parameters in the detailed view of the BOM item. Here, on four tabs, you can enter values such as component scrap, the removal storage location, or extended texts. You can also link documents to the respective BOM item. These can be design drawings or handling instructions.

Values in the material master and bill of material

 Some values in the material master can also be maintained in the BOM item; for example, component scrap. If both fields contain entries, the value in the bill of material takes priority over the value in the material master.

This is always an advantage if the value is different, depending on the use or process. In the case of component scrap, for example, when used in a specific bill of material, the value may be higher than average.

As described in Section 1.3, both the bicycle and the complete frame are new materials. In the previous section, we created the material masters and now we will define the bills of material in the ERP system. To do this, we call up transaction CS01: SAP MENU • LOGISTICS • PRODUCTION • MASTER DATA • BILLS OF MATERIAL • BILL OF MATERIAL • MATERIAL BOM, and enter the material number of the bicycle (*ET-F-WT500*), the number of the plant (*1200*), and the bill of material usage (*1* for "production"). Next, start the transaction by pressing ⌤ Enter . In the item overview that appears, for every BOM item, we maintain the material number of the component, item type L for a stocked material, and the quantity required for our example (see Figure 2.11). The ERP system reads the quantity unit automatically from the material master data of the component once we press ⌤ Enter . The checkmark in the A (assembly) column ❶ shows that there is a bill of material for this item itself—the item is therefore a further assembly. By double-clicking the checkmark, we can go to this bill of material. First, however, we want to look at the header data of the new bill of material. To do this, we click the 📖 icon ❷.

We now check that the base quantity (i.e., the number of bicycles manufactured with the quantities of the BOM items) is exactly 1 (see Figure 2.12), because that is what we drew up the bill of material for. We do not restrict the batch size range valid for this bill of material any further. In the BOM TEXT field, we enter *Bicycle WT500 in the Dresden plant* and in the PLANT field, we enter *1200* for DRESDEN. We can then save and exit the bill of material by clicking 💾.

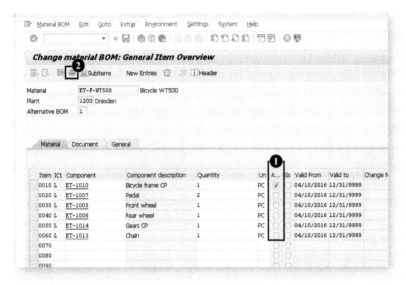

Figure 2.11: Material BOM—Item Overview

Change material BOM: Header Overview

Item | Suom.BOM | Alternative Long Text | BOM Long Text

Material	ET-F-WT500	Bicycle WT500
Plant	1200 Dresden
BOM	00003061
Alternative BOM	1
BOM Usage	1 Production
Technical type	
BOM group	

Quants/long txt | Addnl Data | Admin. data | Doc. assignment

BOM and alternative text

| BOM text | Bicycle WT500 in plant Dresden |
| Alt Text | |

Quantity data

| Base quantity | 1 | PC |

Validity

Change Number		BOM status	1
Valid From	04/10/2016	Authorization group	
Deletion Indicator		Deletion Flag	

Figure 2.12: Material BOM—Header Overview

33

Group BOM

If you create a bill of material without entering a plant, then you create a *group BOM*.

In production planning, however, you cannot use this bill of material due to the missing plant reference. You must first create a plant BOM by calling up transaction CS01 again and, this time, enter a plant. Using the ⬚ button, you can copy the group BOM into the plant BOM so that you do not have to enter all of the information again. If you forget to enter the plant, and thus create a group BOM, a warning message appears in the footer of the screen, drawing your attention to this.

Creating a bill of material

The following video shows how to set up a bill of material in SAP PP: *https://espresso-tutorials.com/PP.php*.

2.3 Work center

In the context of SAP PP, the *work center* describes an organizational unit in which the entire production order or its individual steps are executed. It can be a machine or a manual work center, for example, or a machine group or whole department. It is always assigned to a plant as the higher level organizational unit. In SAP PP, work centers are required in order to describe (in the routing) which employee or which operating resource executes an operation, or where this operation takes place. The work center is also used to link to the SAP modules CO (for cost and activity accounting) and HR (for payroll accounting). To fulfill these functions, the work center contains a number of parameters, as described below.

To fulfill its functions, the work center contains a number of parameters. You define the most important parameters when you create the work center. The work center category (see Figure 2.13) defines, amongst other things, the layout and the work center parameters available. Typical work center categories in the standard SAP system include:

▶ Machine

▶ Machine group

▶ Labor

▶ Person group

Because we do not need any new work centers for the new bicycle, we will look at the existing work center "Welding" in change mode. To do this, we access transaction CR02 from SAP MENU • LOGISTICS • PRODUCTION • MASTER DATA • WORK CENTERS • WORK CENTER. On the selection screen, we enter the plant *1200* and work center *ET-WC-01*.

The BASIC DATA tab (see Figure 2.13) contains details about the person responsible for the work center, the location of the work center, and the task list type (see Section 2.4) in which the work center may be used. The value *009* in the USAGE field means that this work center may be used in all task list types.

The STANDARD VALUE KEY field ❶ is an important one. It defines which activities are decisive for the production on this work center. This information is subsequently used for scheduling, capacity requirements calculations, and cost accounting. We can see here that the work center is a labor work center, is permitted for *All Task List Types*, and covers the three standard values *Setup*, *Machine*, and *Labor*.

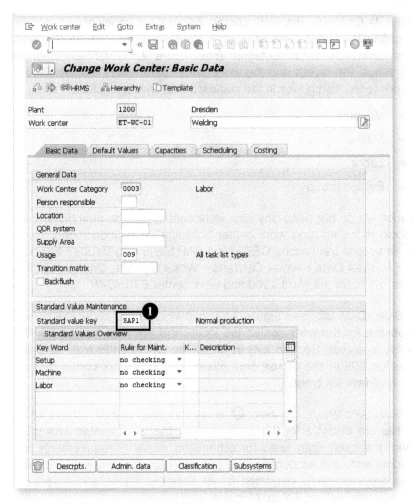

Figure 2.13: Work center—Basic Data view

The DEFAULT VALUES tab (see Figure 2.14) contains various parameters; for example, standard text keys for standard texts or wage types that are automatically proposed when the routings are created in order to reduce the effort involved in creating the master data.

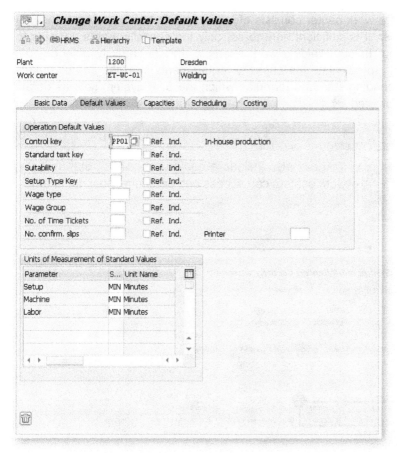

Figure 2.14: Work center tab—Default Values view

On the CAPACITIES tab (see Figure 2.15), you set the category of the work center capacity; you maintain the category via the corresponding function ❶ from the work center or directly via transaction CR12 (see Section 6.2). When you create a new work center, after pressing [Enter] the SAP system automatically switches to the work center capacity view.

Possible capacity categories are:

▶ Machine

▶ Labor

▶ External processing

Even if a work center consists of labor, on one hand, and machines, on the other, it is sufficient here to set only the capacity that is decisive for planning. In our *Welding* work example, this is capacity category *002* (*Labor*). To calculate the capacity requirements from the default values, corresponding standard formulas which the SAP system sets as default were selected ❷ .

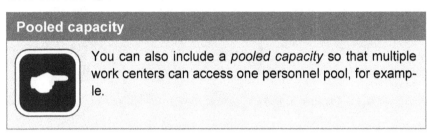

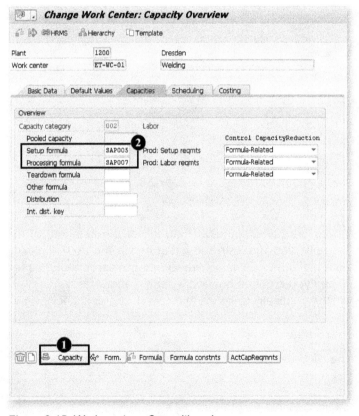

Figure 2.15: Work center—Capacities view

The work center capacity controls the available capacity of the work center. Here, we can set a standard available capacity ❶ or a shift capacity that varies over time ❷. To use the shifts, we select grouping *51*. This key offers both a two-shift plan and a three-shift plan.

In our example, the number of individual capacities (2) indicates that two welders are assigned to this work center; the selection of CAN BE USED BY SEVERAL OPERATIONS defines that these two people can also work on different orders, at the same time. We can see, therefore, that each employee works eight hours each day (not including breaks) and the work center therefore has an available capacity of 16 hours per day. See Figure 2.16.

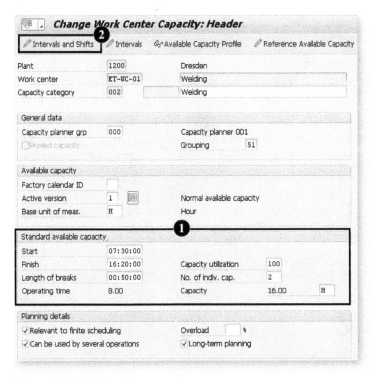

Figure 2.16: Work center capacity

You can regulate how the *execution time* is determined using the settings on the SCHEDULING tab (see Figure 2.17).

Capacity category

 You have to enter the capacity category (in our example *002*) on the SCHEDULING tab because the schedule must be calculated for *precisely one* capacity category. Furthermore, you must also have entered the category on the CAPACITIES tab because the capacity category is a mandatory field; if it does not contain an entry, you cannot exit the SCHEDULING tab.

The settings on the SCHEDULING tab (see Figure 2.17) regulate how the execution time is determined. The capacity category must be entered because this is the basis for the schedule calculation.

Change Work Center: Scheduling

⌂ ⊳ ⊞HRMS ⊞Hierarchy □Template

| Plant | 1200 | Dresden |
| Work center | ET-WC-01 | Welding |

Basic Data | Default Values | Capacities | Scheduling | Costing

Scheduling basis

| Capacity category | 002 | Labor |
| Capacity | | Welding |

Execution time

Duration of Setup	SAP001	i	Prod: Setup time
Processing formula	SAP003	i	Prod: Labor time
Teardown formula			
Other formula			

Interoperation times

| Location Group | | |
| Std. queue time | 6.000 | H | Min. queue time |

Dimension and unit of measure of work

| Work dimension | |
| Work unit | |

🗑 🖨 Capacity | ✂° Form. | 📋 Formula | Formula constnts

Figure 2.17: Work center—Scheduling view

Here too, corresponding formulas must be specified for the calculation. The values in the LOCATION GROUP and STD. QUEUE TIME fields together make up the interoperation time to another work center. Both values have a lower priority compared to the routing. This means that the values from the work center are only used if no values have been maintained in the routing.

Finally, the COSTING tab (see Figure 2.18) contains the links to the modules CO and HR. Here, the work center is assigned to a cost center for the controlling area to which the plant is assigned. Every activity from the standard value key is assigned to an activity type from cost and activity accounting. You also enter the *calculation rule* formula. The INCENTIVE WAGES INDICATOR checkbox is used to select those activities for which an update to the HR module is necessary in order to calculate wages.

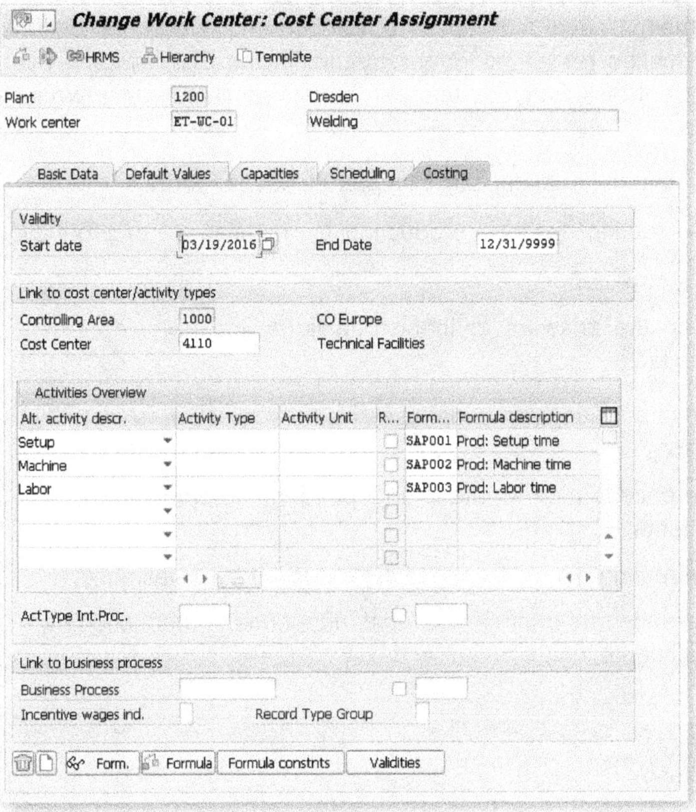

Figure 2.18: Work center—Costing view

Creating a work center

 In SAP PP, the work center is the central organizational unit within a plant for executing a production order. For information about how to create a work center, see the following video: *https://espresso-tutorials.com/PP.php*.

2.4 Routing

Routings are the most important master data for production. They describe what has to be done, where it has to be done, and in what order, in order to produce a product. They also contain information about the duration of the individual activities, the required employee qualifications, and the production resources/tools required. In the SAP system, there are four different task list types that can be differentiated using two simple questions:

1. Is the routing material-specific or material-independent?

2. Does the routing describe production by installments or production by lot size?

Depending on the answers to these questions, the following task list types are available:

▶ Standard routing—material-specific, no production by installments

▶ Reference routing—material-independent, no production by installments

▶ Rate routing—material-specific, production by installments

▶ Reference rate routing—material-independent, production by installments

The *standard routing* is the most common routing type. It describes the process flows for discrete production of exactly one material. You can create multiple standard routings for the material in one task list group, because different process flows can apply for certain lot size ranges. A standard routing can also include reference routings.

A *reference routing* describes typical recurring and material-independent production steps. If standard routings contain references to a reference routing, you only have to change the reference routing to update the standard routings for all materials. Both routing types can be merged into task list groups and consist of sequences and operations.

For *rate* and *reference rate routings* the same applies, the difference being that these routings are designed specifically for planning with specific production rates; for example, 10,000 pieces per shift. The routings are set up in the SAP system using the structure shown in Figure 2.19.

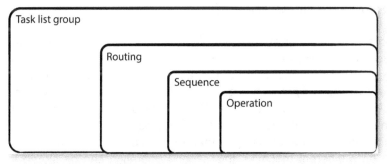

Figure 2.19: Structure of routings

The header of a routing (see Figure 2.20) contains particular organizational data. As a routing is plant-specific, the header contains the plant for which the routing applies. Further values to be entered are the task list usage, the status of the routing, and the planner group; i.e., the key figure for the person(s) responsible for this routing.

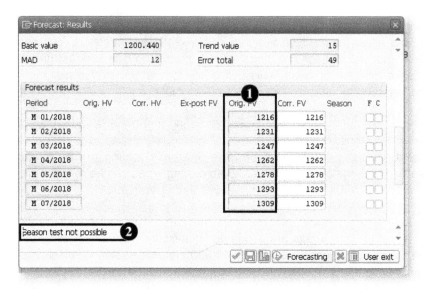

Figure 2.20: Standard routing, header detail

Each routing consists of at least one *sequence*, known as the *standard sequence*. This is created automatically when you create the routing. The sequence is the linear order of processes that are executed to manufacture a product. If production steps for a product run in parallel, they are assigned to a *parallel sequence*. The parallel sequence is always an additional "branch" of the routing and is executed in every case. If there is an alternative to one or more of these operations, for example, processing on a different machine, this second operation can be stored in an *alternative sequence*. Both types of sequence are linked to the standard sequence entered by the work scheduler via a relationship. The alternative sequence is selected for an order when required and replaces the section of the standard sequence defined by the relationship.

The *operation* then contains all information for executing the production operation: the name of the work center that executes the production step, an activity description, and the predefined activity quantity. The standard value key for the work center entered determines which activities are planned and required. Each operation is also assigned a control key. This value defines the processing in the subsequent process and controls whether the operation is processed in-house or externally, whether it creates capacity requirements, whether it is scheduled with all other operations, or whether it is merely a text item.

In our bicycle example, the work scheduler now has to create a routing for all new parts produced in-house. These are: the frame, the fork, and the CP (= complete) frame. A routing is also required for the assembly of the completed bicycle. Both the frame and the fork are manufactured from aluminum pipes of different diameters. These are delivered in the correct length and welded together on-site. The work scheduler creates the first operation for the material ET-1011 FRAME with the work center ET-WC-01 WELDING. The control key of the latter from the DEFAULT VALUES tab is entered in the routing. Under DESCRIPTION, the work scheduler names the activity to be completed (see Figure 2.21).

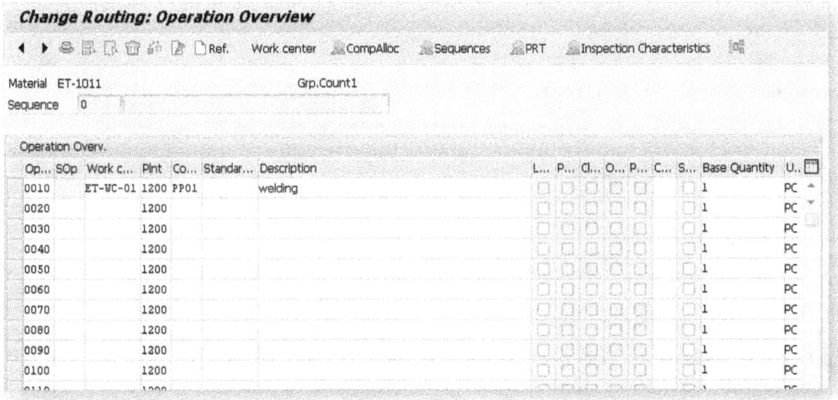

Figure 2.21: Standard routing, operation overview

By double-clicking the operation number, you can display the details of the operation to enter further input (see Figure 2.22). To prepare the work center, *30* minutes must be scheduled, and the work scheduler enters this under SETUP. The actual processing time should be *20* minutes, and this time is entered in the LABOR field. As the *Welding* work center does not contain any machines, no machine time has to be maintained.

After welding, the frame has to cool down for one hour before further steps can be executed. The work scheduler therefore enters a process-related wait time in the routing (see Figure 2.23). This is taken into account in the scheduling before transporting to the next work center.

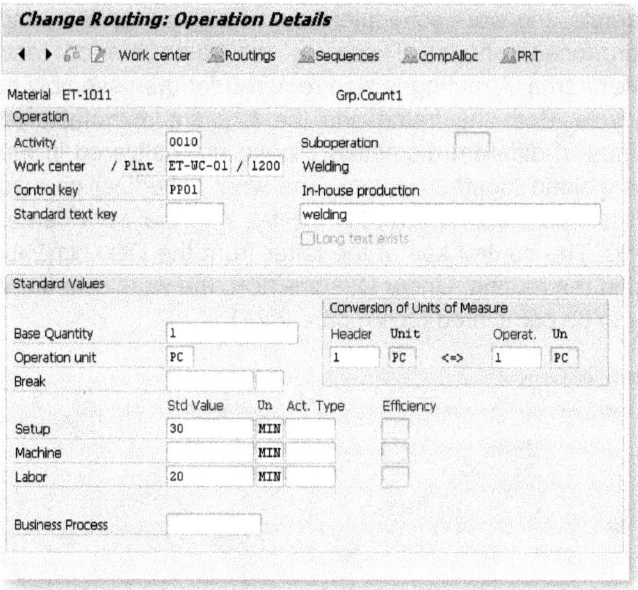

Change Routing: Operation Details

◀ ▶ ⌂ 📝 Work center 🔷Routings 🔷Sequences 🔷CompAlloc 🔷PRT

Material ET-1011   Grp.Count1

Operation

Activity	0010	Suboperation	
Work center / Plnt	ET-WC-01 / 1200	Welding	
Control key	PP01	In-house production	
Standard text key		welding	
		☐ Long text exists	

Standard Values

		Conversion of Units of Measure				
		Header	Unit		Operat.	Un
Base Quantity	1	1	PC	<=>	1	PC
Operation unit	PC					
Break						

	Std Value	Un	Act. Type	Efficiency
Setup	30	MIN		
Machine		MIN		
Labor	20	MIN		

Business Process

Figure 2.22: Operation detail, standard values

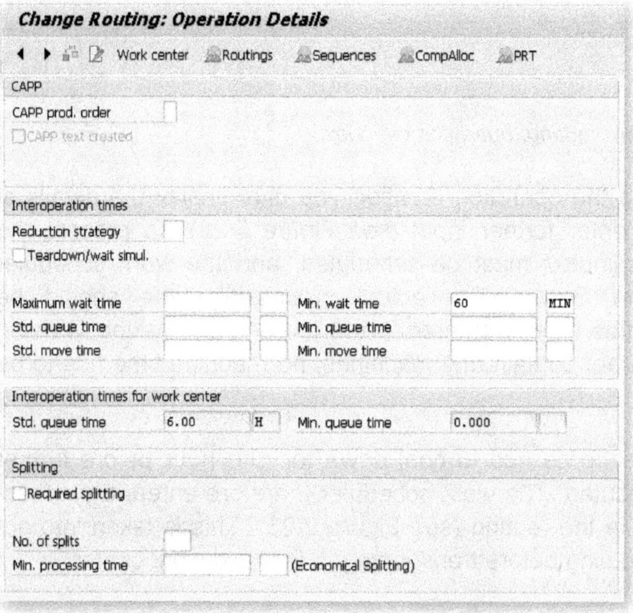

Change Routing: Operation Details

◀ ▶ ⌂ 📝 Work center 🔷Routings 🔷Sequences 🔷CompAlloc 🔷PRT

CAPP

CAPP prod. order ☐
☐ CAPP text created

Interoperation times

Reduction strategy ☐
☐ Teardown/wait simul.

Maximum wait time		Min. wait time	60	MIN
Std. queue time		Min. queue time		
Std. move time		Min. move time		

Interoperation times for work center

Std. queue time	6.00	H	Min. queue time	0.000

Splitting

☐ Required splitting

No. of splits ☐
Min. processing time ☐ (Economical Splitting)

Figure 2.23: Operation detail, transition values

The work scheduler repeats this procedure for all operations required to manufacture the frame. After welding, the frame is painted with a base coat and a color.

The work scheduler also creates further routings for the fork and the complete frame. Bills of material for the frame and the fork must also be created, because the designer has not been able to create these. The bills of material can only be written once the plans have been designed and the original material requirements defined. In addition to the aluminum pipe sections required, the bills of material contain details about the paint for the frame and the fork.

Because not all the items on the bill of material are required for the welding, the work scheduler assigns the components. To do this, transaction CA02 is called up in order to open the routing again and the [F7] key is used, jumping to the COMPONENT ASSIGNMENT. By clicking the buttons to the left of the line (see ❶ in Figure 2.24), the first and second items are selected, and by clicking NEW ASSIGNMENT ❷ (or pressing the [F5] key), the items are assigned to OPERATION 0010 (❸). In the same way, the base coat is assigned to operation 0020 and the blue paint to operation 0030.

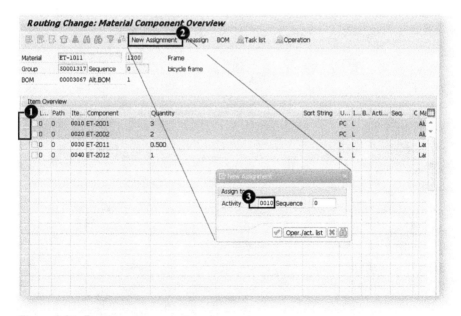

Figure 2.24: Routing, component assignment

All the master data required for production planning has now been created. The material master records with the relevant views, the bills of material, and the work centers and routings can now be used to determine the quantities required to cover sales order requirements or planned requirement quantities, and to control and monitor procurement or manufacturing. In the next chapter, we will look at how to determine the planned requirement quantities as part of sales and operations planning.

Creating a routing

 The routings contain the most important master data for a production order. They should be created with great care, as you can see in the video "Creating a Routing": *https://espresso-tutorials.com/PP.php*

3 Sales and Operations Planning

Record your planned sales, plan with multiple hierarchy levels, determine the resources required, and compare this planning to the resources available.

With Sales and Operations Planning, SAP SE provides a standard version of these activities. This standard version works only with product group hierarchies and a predefined set of key figures. The layout of the planning table is also preconfigured and can therefore be used straight "out of the box".

Compared to the standard version of SOP, the *Flexible Planning* component offers greater freedom with regard to structuring your data, the key figures to be planned, and the layout of the planning table. In the following section, I outline the Sales and Operations Planning (SOP) processes using standard SOP and explain the basic principles of these processes. Rough-cut planning is easy to use and does not require any extensive customizing prior to use. Based on this preliminary work, in Chapter 4 we will be able to determine the production and procurement quantities.

3.1 Product groups

As previously explained in Section 1.1, sales and operations planning in SAP ERP takes place at an aggregated level. To perform this planning, you have to define certain *hierarchies* which you can then use to aggregate the sales figures. These hierarchies can be customer hierarchies by sales region or product groups, for example. SAP ERP also supports multiple aggregation levels. In the following section, I will stick to product groups as the standard SOP hierarchy.

Product groups are simple data structures. They consist of a header and components. The data in the header provides information about the name of the product group, the designation of the product group, the plant, and the quantity unit in which this product group is planned. In addition to the material number, the components include the key for the plant, the quantity unit required, and a proportional factor which describes the distribution of the components within the product group.

To ensure that the planned quantity of the entire product group can be distributed to the materials which belong to the product group, the percentage ratio of each material to the overall quantity of materials must be known to the system. There are two basic approaches for obtaining information about this percentage ratio:

▶ It can be estimated by sales experts for the next planning period.

▶ It is calculated based on actual past consumption quantities.

In practice, of course, the ratio can be initially calculated from the historical data, and then adjusted by experts according to expectations for the future.

Product groups relevant for MRP

 When SOP is transferred to demand management, the system checks whether a material appears in multiple product groups and whether one product group is marked as the one relevant for MRP. There can only be *one* such product group for each material; this prevents the material receiving requirements from multiple product groups.

You set the corresponding indicator for each component individually in the product group.

In our example, we have developed a new bicycle. To plan the sales figures, we add the material number to the existing product group. To do this, we call up transaction MC86 (Change Product Group) either directly or via the SAP menu: LOGISTICS • PRODUCTION • SOP • PRODUCT GROUP. On the selection screen (see Figure 3.1), and we enter the name of the product group (in our case, *ET-F-W*) and the plant (*1200*) in which the product group is planned.

The screen in Figure 3.2 shows the previous composition of the product group. In the upper part of the view, we can see the header data of the product group and in the lower part, the data for the individual components.

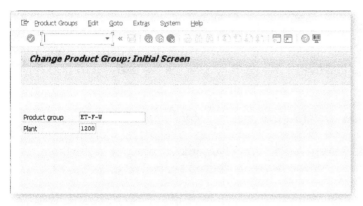

Figure 3.1: Selecting the product group

We can see that our product group previously comprised three bicycles ❶ and in the last round of planning, the sales department assumed a distribution of 40/20/40 ❷. In this view, we add the material number of the new bicycle (*ET-F-WT500*, see Figure 3.3) and then calculate the ratio.

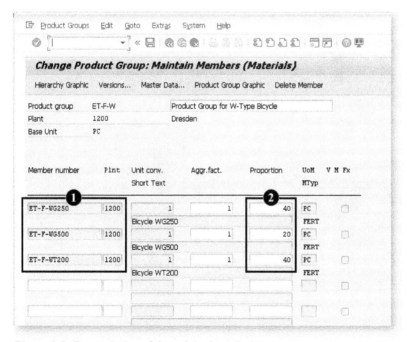

Figure 3.2: Presentation of the original product group

To do this, via the menu item EDIT, we select the PROPORTION CALCULA-
TION function. In the dialog box that opens, the system prompts us to
enter the precise period to be analyzed in order to determine the ratio.
We select the last twelve months and execute the analysis by clicking ✅
.

The SAP ERP system now uses the consumption values of the four
items in the product group to determine the actual individual material
percentages of the sales for the entire product group. For the three "old"
materials, the system shows a distribution of 35/40/25.

Our new bicycle received a percentage of "0" because we have not
posted any quantities yet. The sales department has informed us that it
expects the new bicycle to achieve a 20% market share within the product group, with a uniform reduction in the percentages of the old items.
We therefore enter the new distribution *28/32/20/20* in the product group
(see Figure 3.3) and save it by clicking 💾. This completes the mainte-
nance of the product group.

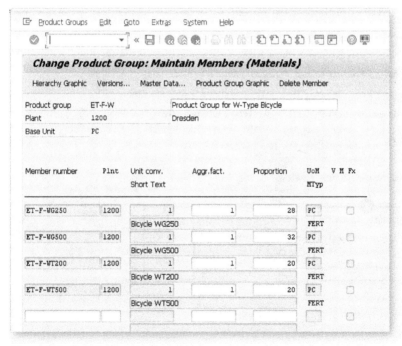

Figure 3.3: Updated product group

3.2   Rough-cut planning profile

In Section 1.1, I showed you that in the MRP II concept according to Sales and Operations Planning, a check of the resources should guarantee that the planning can be implemented. Also in this planning step, the basis for the analysis is the comparison of the capacity requirements and the available capacity. In SAP ERP, the latter is read from the work center data (see Section 2.3). The capacity requirements, however, are recorded using the *rough-cut planning profiles*.

Compared to the more detailed routings, the rough-cut planning profiles are very simple data structures which enable us to plan on an aggregated view. For this purpose, work center capacities, materials (usually raw materials), production resources/tools, or direct costs are available as planning bottlenecks to be taken into consideration. Because this planning is rough-cut planning, in contrast to the capacity planning discussed in Chapter 6, we do not precisely plan to the minute and second, or to individual work centers, but rather to work center groups.

The profile consists of a simple table. The individual columns contain the periods for which requirements are being recorded—the periods could be workdays, for example, or calendar weeks. The rows contain all resources that we require, across all bill of material levels, to manufacture the material or the product group.

Task list usage	
	If you want to use work centers or work center groups, make sure that the task list usage for the work centers allows use in rough-cut planning profiles (see Section 2.3)!

We will now create a new rough-cut planning profile for our product group ET-F-W. To do this, we call up transaction MC35 via the path: SAP MENU • LOGISTICS • PRODUCTION • SOP • TOOLS • ROUGH-CUT PLANNING PROFILE. On the selection screen, we enter values in the PRODUCT GROUP and PLANT fields, and click EXECUTE ❶ (see Figure 3.4).

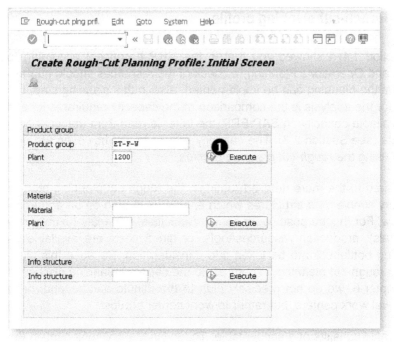

Figure 3.4: Rough-cut planning profile selection screen

Further rough-cut planning profiles

 You use the same transaction to create rough-cut planning profiles for materials, and for flexible planning. Enter your data in the corresponding area of the selection screen and use the button assigned to execute the procedure.

A dialog box opens and we enter the general data for the profile (see Figure 3.5). The value in the TIME SPAN field ❶ controls how many WORKDAYS are combined for a period (i.e., into one column in the table). The value in the BASE QUANTITY field ❷ corresponds to the base quantity that we define resource requirements for in the table. The fields for the selection data ❸ will already be familiar to you from the routing (see Section 2.4) and are also filled accordingly. By clicking ✔ (continue button), we access the actual rough-cut planning profile.

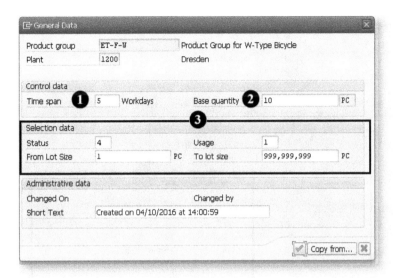

Figure 3.5: Rough-cut planning profile, general data

We now see the periods defined in the columns (see Figure 3.6); in the individual rows we can enter the resources required for the rough-cut planning. For our product group, these are the *Assembly* and *Paint shop* work center groups. Double-click the field in the first column ❶. In the dialog box that opens ❷, we enter a name for the resource (in our example, *Paint shop*) and as resource type, we select the WORK CENTER checkbox. In the second dialog box ❸, which appears after we click the green checkmark ✓ (hidden in the image), we enter the actual work center *ET-WC-02*, the plant *1200*, and the unit for the work *H* (hour). We close all the dialog boxes by clicking ✓ and then repeat these steps for the second work center.

Because there is a period of approximately one week between the work steps on these two work centers, we enter the capacity requirements in hours for the paint shop in the first column, and the requirements for assembly in the second column (see ❶ in Figure 3.7). Once we have entered the information, we can save it by clicking 🖫.

We have now created a rough-cut planning profile that we can use to subject the planned production quantities to a *capacity analysis*.

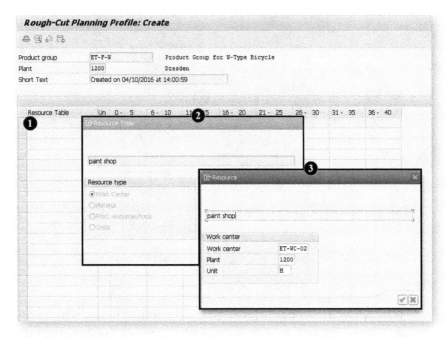

Figure 3.6: Integrating a resource in a rough-cut planning profile

Figure 3.7: Resource requirements in a rough-cut planning profile

3.3   Standard SOP

With standard planning, SAP provides a preconfigured *planning book* for planning sales and production quantities, as well as stocks.

As described in the introduction to this chapter, standard SOP uses a simple planning table with six defined key figures. Four of these—SALES, PRODUCTION, TARGET STOCK LEVEL, and TARGET DAY'S SUPPLY—can be changed. The key figures WAREHOUSE STOCK and RANGE OF COVERAGE are calculated automatically from the sales and production.

There are several options for determining the *sales figures*. The easiest option would logically be to enter the planned values in the table **manually**. However, the SAP system offers alternatives for generating or transferring the data. If sales planning has already been performed in the **sales information system** or in **CO-PA**, you can transfer the values directly from there.

You can also have the system **forecast** the sales figures based on historical data. If you decide to do this, you can select between different forecast models: constant models, seasonal models, trend models, and seasonal trend models (see Figure 3.10).

SAP ERP can also support you in generating the *production quantities*. The standard SOP makes you decide whether to plan synchronously with sales, or plan so that you achieve a predefined target stock level or a target days' supply.

Ultimately, *capacity leveling* allows you to display the resource consumption for the planned production quantity and compare it with the resources available. If there are capacity overloads, you can identify them and take appropriate measures such as adjusting the production quantities and improving the capacity available, seeing as the planning is long-term.

In Sections 3.1 and 3.2 we laid the foundations for SOP. We now want to perform the actual planning for our product group. Because we have the active plan scenario from the last planning cycle, we start transaction MC82 from the menu: LOGISTICS • PRODUCTION • SOP • PLANNING • FOR PRODUCT GROUP.

On the selection screen, we enter our product group *ET-F-W* and the plant *1200,* and click ACTIVE VERSION ❶ (see Figure 3.8).

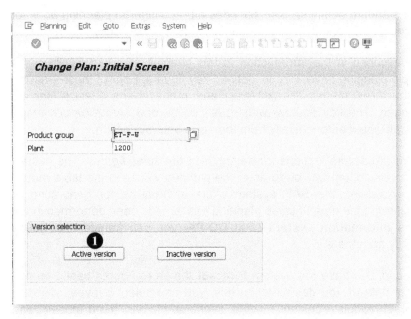

Figure 3.8: Initial screen for the standard SOP

Inactive version

 Standard SOP allows you to plan in multiple versions and to check and compare these plans. To do this, you create inactive versions; in contrast to the active version, you can have any number of inactive versions. The recommendation is to use the inactive versions to test different scenarios and then copy the approved and agreed scenarios to the active version A00.

We are now in the planning table of standard SOP (see Figure 3.9). In the header ❶, we see the name of the product group, the plant, and the version that we are performing the planning for. Below this ❷, is the detail area in which the planning key figures and planning periods are displayed.

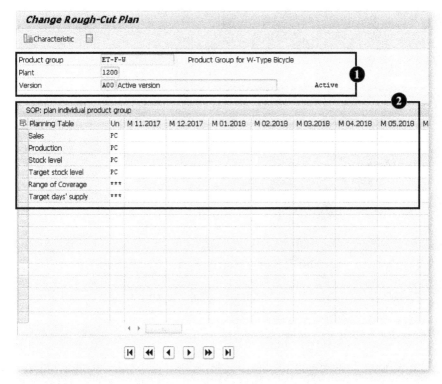

Figure 3.9: Standard SOP planning table

You can access the most important functions for planning via the menu: EDIT • CREATE SALES PLAN and EDIT • CREATE PRODUCTN PLAN. In our example, there is no preliminary planning that we can adopt. Therefore, we initially use a forecast as the basis for planning.

We start the *forecast* via: EDIT • CREATE SALES PLAN • FORECAST... and in a dialog box (see Figure 3.10), the system prompts us to select the model.

First, we enter the period intervals ❶ for the forecast and the historical data. We allow SAP ERP to select the most suitable forecast model by selecting AUTOMATIC MODEL SELECTION ❷, under FORECAST EXECUTION. By clicking the HISTORICAL... button at the bottom of the dialog box, we can then display the desired number of historical values.

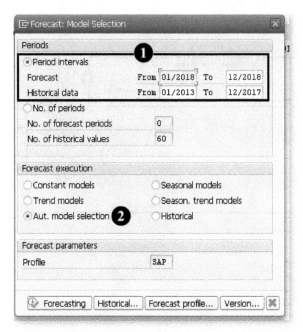

Figure 3.10: Forecast—model selection

The window that opens usually displays the historical consumption values (see Figure 3.11). We can check these values for outliers (i.e., values that deviate significantly from the average) that have a negative impact on our forecast. Outliers can arise due to delivery bottlenecks or one-time large orders. Because there were no past consumption values here, I have entered all values as corrected values so that we get a result from the forecast.

We exit this window by clicking FORECASTING.

In the next step, we start the forecast. Another window appears for the model selection (see Figure 3.12). Here we confirm the SAP system proposal for testing by TREND AND SEASON. We also exit this window by clicking FORECASTING or by pressing [F8].

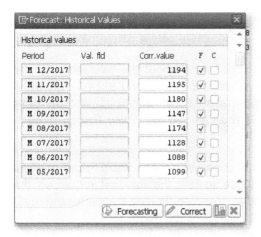

Figure 3.11: Forecast history

Figure 3.12: Forecast—parameters for automatic model selection

We now see the results of the forecast in a further dialog box (see Figure 3.13 and Figure 3.14).

The header data ❶ contains information about the evaluation of the forecast; in our case, the basic value of the forecast *1200.400*, the trend value *15*, the MAD (median of the absolute deviation) *12*, and the error total of the ex-post forecast *49*. You can use these key figures to compare two forecasts.

The details ❷ show the consumption values and the *ex-post forecast values* for the past. We use these to test the forecast model on the known values from the past and to calculate the key figures for the MAD and ERROR TOTAL fields.

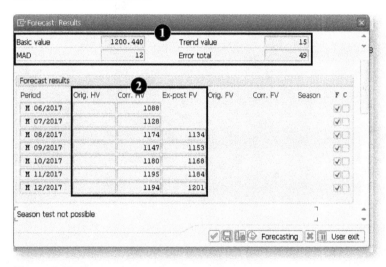

Figure 3.13: Forecast—results, ex-post forecast

If we scroll down (see Figure 3.14), we see the forecast values ❶ for the forecast interval entered in Figure 3.10. If necessary, we can also correct these manually by entering values in the CORR. FV column.

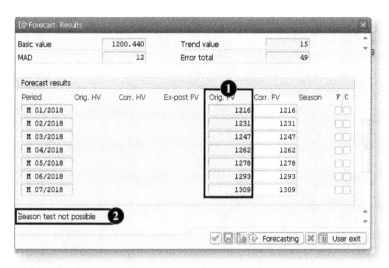

Figure 3.14: Forecast results

Below the details is a text line about the time series characteristic which has changed ❷. When we double-click this line, the *procedural and error message log* for the forecast opens (see Figure 3.15). This log contains all messages created during the program run. We close the log again, and because we are satisfied with the results, we accept them by clicking the green checkmark ✔, as shown in Figure 3.14.

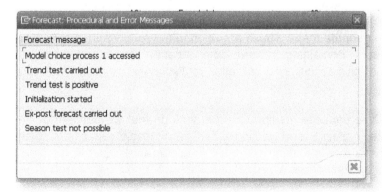

Figure 3.15: Forecast—procedural and error messages

The values have now been transferred to the SALES key figure. Now, to add the production quantities, we select the menu item: EDIT • CREATE PRODUCTN PLAN • SYNCHRONOUS TO SALES. The sales quantities are adopted 1:1 as production quantities. Our planning book now shows sales and production figures (see Figure 3.16).

Change Rough-Cut Plan

Characteristic

Product group	ET-F-W		Product Group for W-Type Bicycle				
Plant	1200						
Version	A00 Active version				Active		

SOP: plan individual product group

Planning Table	Un	M 01/2018	M 02/2018	M 03/2018	M 04/2018	M 05/2018	M 06/2018	M 07/2018
Sales	PC	1216	1231	1247	1262	1278	1293	1309
Production	PC	1216	1231	1247	1262	1278	1293	1309
Stock level	PC							
Target stock level	PC							
Range of Coverage	***							
Target days' supply	***							

Figure 3.16: Planning table with sales and production quantities

However, we do not know yet whether this production is actually feasible, and we therefore start the capacity evaluation by selecting the menu item: VIEWS • CAPACITY SITUATION • ROUGH-CUT PLANNING • SHOW. Beneath our planning table, we now see the table with the resource load. For every resource that we have specified in the rough-cut planning profile, a section containing the available capacity, the capacity requirements, and the capacity load utilization is displayed, as shown in Figure 3.17.

The *available capacity* results from the settings that we defined for the work center capacity (see Section 2.3). The available capacity is determined for the monthly planning period in accordance with the work calendar that applies for the plant.

For the *capacity requirements*, the rough-cut planning profile is simply multiplied by the planned production quantity and set in the capacity load utilization with reference to the available capacity.

If we look at the *capacity load utilization*, it becomes clear that, in principle, there is sufficient capacity available at work center ET-WC-03 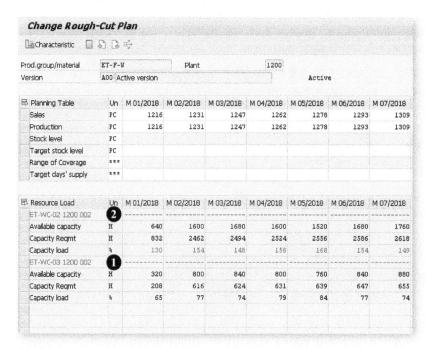 (paint shop). However, the assembly (work center ET-WC-02 ❷) cannot cope with the planned quantities due to the limited capacity available. The capacity load utilization is at (up to) 168%. We have multiple options for solving the problem:

▶ The first option is to reduce the sales quantity; this is probably the least practicable solution as it would mean a loss of sales.

▶ An alternative would be to bring production forward to meet the higher expected sales from the warehouse stock; however, this solution works only for sales peaks over a limited time.

▶ The third variant involves increasing the available capacity by setting up a further work center or a further shift on the existing work centers.

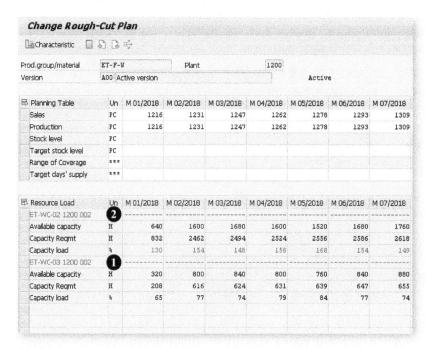

Change Rough-Cut Plan

Characteristic

| Prod.group/material | ET-F-W | | Plant | | 1200 | | |
| Version | A00 | Active version | | | Active | | |

Planning Table	Un	M 01/2018	M 02/2018	M 03/2018	M 04/2018	M 05/2018	M 06/2018	M 07/2018
Sales	PC	1216	1231	1247	1262	1278	1293	1309
Production	PC	1216	1231	1247	1262	1278	1293	1309
Stock level	PC							
Target stock level	PC							
Range of Coverage	***							
Target days' supply	***							

Resource Load	Un	M 01/2018	M 02/2018	M 03/2018	M 04/2018	M 05/2018	M 06/2018	M 07/2018
ET-WC-02 1200 002 ❷								
Available capacity	H	640	1600	1680	1600	1520	1680	1760
Capacity Reqmt	H	832	2462	2494	2524	2556	2586	2618
Capacity load	%	130	154	148	158	168	154	149
ET-WC-03 1200 002 ❶								
Available capacity	H	320	800	840	800	760	840	880
Capacity Reqmt	H	208	616	624	631	639	647	655
Capacity load	%	65	77	74	79	84	77	74

Figure 3.17: Planning table with resource load

3.4   Disaggregation and transferring requirements

The production figures are still in a rough breakdown in the SOP structures. To allow you to work with these figures further in the requirements
planning, they have to be distributed via demand management to the
level of "material per plant". In some circumstances, a breakdown over
weeks or days is also shown.

SAP ERP can also help you with this task. For the *hierarchical apportionment of the quantities*, the proportional factor from the product group
is used. This allows you to transfer the quantities available at the product
group level to the level of the individual material.

As we have seen, in a product group, you can enter information for a
material in two different plants and thus effect an apportionment of quantities over two or more plants. The best way to start this task is from SOP
with transaction MC75 (Transfer of Planning Data to Demand Management). You can also access it via the path: SAP MENU • LOGISTICS • PRO-
DUCTION • SOP • DISAGGREGATION.

Temporal apportionment of planned quantities

 The requirement for a temporal disaggregation is based
on the *planning scenario* and the *production frequency*.
For example, if the product is produced several times
per month, but the requirements are only transferred to
the requirements planning on a monthly basis, the requirements planning will not be able to generate a realistic procurement
proposal.

SAP ERP supports the temporal apportionment to the effect that distribution always takes place using workdays. For a distribution of months to
weeks, this ensures that this distribution is correct, even if the change of
month does not fall precisely with the change of week. An apportionment
over days is also possible without any problem. The factory calendar of
the plant is always used, meaning that in the disaggregation, you are not
limited to a five-day week and if necessary, you can distribute over all of
the days defined as workdays in your business.

We will now distribute our product group planning which we created in this chapter and for which we have checked the resource situation at material/plant level and over weeks. To do this, we call up transaction MC75. On the selection screen, we enter our product group *ET-F-W*, the plant *1200*, and the plan version *A00* ❶ (see Figure 3.18).

In the TRANSFER STRATEGY AND PERIOD area ❷, we select PRODUCTION PLAN FOR MATERIAL(S) OR PG MEMBERS AS PROPORTION OF PG. We set the transfer period ❸ in accordance with our planning scenario. We then run the transaction by clicking TRANSFER NOW ❹.

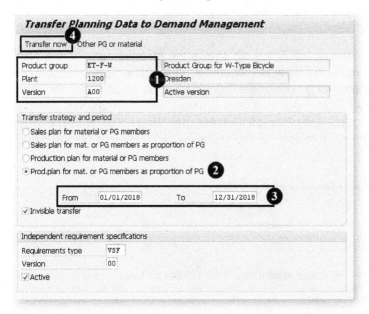

Figure 3.18: Transferring planning data to demand management

Temporal apportionment within SOP

In principle, the disaggregation option is also available in SOP. However, the planned values are then still only components of SOP and are not visible for the material requirements planning. I will therefore describe the procedure with the transfer to the material requirements planning.

To verify the success of the transfer, we open the planned independent requirements with transaction MD62 (Change Planned Independent Requirements) via the path: LOGISTICS • PRODUCTION • MASTER PLANNING • DEMAND MANAGEMENT • PLANNED INDEPENDENT REQUIREMENTS.

We start the transaction with our product group, the plant, and by selecting ALL ACTIVE VERSIONS. A planning table is displayed again—the table for demand management (see Figure 3.19).

In the header data we see the product group and planning period selected. The detail area consists of three different tabs: TABLE, ITEMS, and SCHEDULE LINES.

In the first columns, the TABLE tab shows the material number, the plant or planning area, the version (column V), the active flag, and the base quantity (column BU). These are followed by the columns for the planning periods. These columns are dynamic and can display months, weeks and days. A mixture of all these periods is also possible if, for example, you want to look at two materials with different planning periods.

Plnd Ind. Reqmts Change: Planning Table

Product group   ET-F-W   Product Group for W-Type Bicycle
Planning start   01/02/2018   Planning End   12/31/2018

Table   Items   Sched. Lines

Material	MRP ...	V	A	BU	M 01/2018	M 02/2018	M 03/2018	M 04/2018	M 05/2018	M 06/2018	M 07/2018	M 08/2
ET-F-WG250	00	00	✓	PC	340	345	349	353	358	362	367	
ET-F-WG500	1200	00	✓	PC	389	394	399	404	409	414	419	
ET-F-WT200	1200	00	✓	PC	243	246	249	252	256	259	262	
ET-F-WT500	1200	00	✓	PC	243	246	249	252	256	259	262	
		00	✓									
		00	✓									
		00	✓									

Figure 3.19: Planned independent requirements, demand management table

On the ITEMS tab page, the relevant *control parameters* are displayed for each material (see Figure 3.20). The requirements plan and the planned quantity result from the demand management planning table. The requirements type and the consumption control the behavior of the planned independent requirements. The following values are purely informative and are maintained in the material master:

- ▶ Strategy group
- ▶ MRP type
- ▶ MRP group
- ▶ MRP controller

PInd Ind. Reqmts Change: Item Screen

Material	Short Text	MRP ...	V	A	Req Plan	Plan Qty	BU	RTyp	CI	S...	M...	MRP...	M...	S	H	T..
ET-F-WG250	Bicycle WG250	1200	00	✓		3,625	PC	VSF	1	40	ND	0031		✓	✓	
ET-F-WG500	Bicycle WG500	1200	00	✓		4,144	PC	VSF	1	40	ND	0031		✓	✓	
ET-F-WT200	Bicycle WT200	1200	00	✓		2,589	PC	VSF	1	40	ND	0031		✓	✓	
ET-F-WT500	Bicycle WT500	1200	00	✓		2,589	PC	VSF	1	40	PD	0031	000	✓	✓	
			00	✓												
			00	✓												
			00	✓												

Product group   ET-F-W   Product Group for W-Type Bicycle
Planning start   01/02/2018 Planning End   12/31/2018
Table Items Sched. Lines

Figure 3.20: Demand management items

Requirements plan

The REQUIREMENTS PLAN field offers you further opportunity to classify the planned requirement quantities. In the pure text field, when you create the planned independent requirements, you can enter any information you like. This key then identifies your requirements within the higher-level version and is also displayed as a text for the MRP element in the stock/requirements list (see Section 4.4).

The SCHEDULE LINES tab (see Figure 3.21) shows the demand schedule lines created for each item. This view has a separate header area in which the control parameters for the selected material are again displayed. This is followed by the detail area where every schedule line is listed with the period indicator (month, week, day), the requirements date, and the planned quantity. The column highlighted in this detail area ❶ allows different key figures to be displayed.

If you click the SCHEDULES LINES tab and withdrawals have already taken place, the *withdrawal quantity* of the item is displayed. This is the quantity that was offset with a requirement element (usually a customer order) and for which a *goods issue* has consequently been posted. When the goods issue is posted, the planned quantity is reduced and added as a withdrawal quantity.

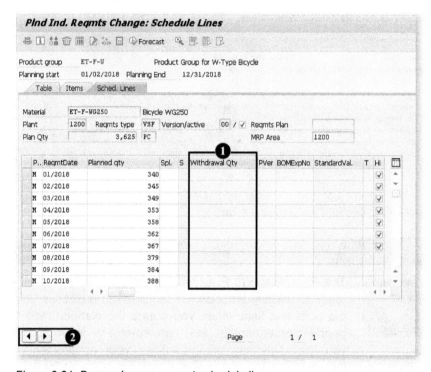

Figure 3.21: Demand management schedule lines

The *item value* is the monetary value of the planned quantity which has been valued with the price from the accounting view of the material master.

You can switch between the two key figures by selecting WITHDRAWAL QUANTITY <-->VALUES in the SETTINGS menu.

A further key figure that you can display in this column is the *calculated quantity*. This has already been assigned to a specific requirements element and is calculated automatically (controlled by the material master settings in the MRP 3 view) with this element in the requirements planning. The planned quantity itself is adjusted with the first goods issue (see above). You can display the calculated quantity key figure via the menu item SETTINGS • CALCULATED QUANTITY.

Below the detail area are the buttons that you can use to navigate through the individual items ❷.

Planning with a production version or serial number

 You can define specific requirements for a schedule line according to a certain production version (PVER) or serial number. The corresponding columns are located in the schedule line view (see Figure 3.21). You activate the columns via the corresponding functions in the SETTINGS menu. If you do define such specifications, they are taken into account in the subsequent requirements planning and corresponding planned orders are created.

Several options are available in demand management for allocating the requirements on a time basis; for example, in the schedule line view, in the SPLIT column, you can enter a period indicator such as the month (*M*), week (*W*), or day format (*D*). Once you press the ⌜Enter⌟ key, SAP ERP automatically apportions the schedule line quantity to the new periods, as shown in Figure 3.22. Here, the planned quantity for December has been allocated over weeks.

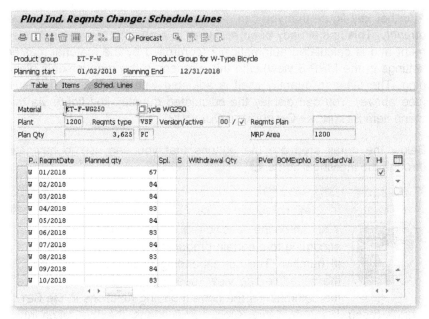

Figure 3.22: Demand management schedule lines allocated over weeks

3.5 Summary

In this chapter, we have learned how to process sales and operations planning in SAP ERP. Based on the sales figures that we receive—regardless of whether we receive them on paper, in an Excel file, or from other SAP modules—we were able to derive a rough master production schedule. We have checked this plan for feasibility using a rough-cut planning profile and then transferred the production figures of the product group to individual materials in order to then transfer them to requirements planning as planned requirement quantities. The subsequent requirements planning steps are covered in the next chapter.

4 Materials planning

When a requirement is recorded or created in a company, SAP ERP plans the production and procurement of this item from the end product to the raw material.

4.1 Requirements

Following on from the information in Chapter 2, in SAP ERP there are also several requirements: *independent requirements, dependent requirements,* and *tertiary requirements.* There are also *additional requirements*: these should cover scrap, wear and tear, shrinkage, and waste, and are applied to the other requirements as a percentage. In general, however, only the independent and dependent requirements are planned.

For each requirements type, SAP includes different MRP elements that define the origin of the requirement in more detail, depending on the business process. The independent requirements include the customer requirements (CusReq), the independent requirements (IndReq), and the forecast requirements (ForReq). In most organizations, the sales organization records the independent requirements and makes them available to the planning department via SAP ERP.

The dependent requirements are differentiated between dependent requirements from planned orders (DepReq) and order reservations from production orders (OrdRes). The DepReq arise from the existing planning and therefore can also be changed by the material requirements planning.

4.2 Planned orders

Planned orders are simply constructed elements of material requirements planning (see Figure 4.1). Their most important function is to transfer requirement quantities along the production levels. They therefore contain, at a minimum, details of the order quantity, the basic dates, and a bill of material ❶. Further elements include the date for which the material will probably be available and the code of the production plant.

Display Planned Order: Stock order

❶

🔧 Components | 📄 Components

Stock order	▾ 37919	Standard in-house pr... ▾	
Material	ET-F-WT500	🗂 ycle WT500	
MRP Area	1200	Dresden	

Header | Assignment | Master Data

Quantities

Order quantity	246	PC	Scrap quantity	0

Dates/Times

	Basic Dates	Production Dates	Other Dates	
End	01/31/2018	00:00:00	Available for MRP	02/01/2018
Start	01/29/2018	00:00:00	GR processing time	1
Opening	01/15/2018			

Other Data

		Firming
Production Plant	1200	☐ Planned Order
Storage Location		☐ Components
Production Version		☐ Capacity Dispatched
BOM Explosion Number		
		☑ Conversion Indicator

Figure 4.1: Displaying a planned order, header data

The lead time for a planned order (i.e., the interval between the basic finish date and the basic start date) results from the in-house production time defined in the material master. From this information, the requirements date by which the components have to be available can be calculated. You can find this in the COMPONENT OVERVIEW of the planned order (see ❶ in Figure 4.2).

Processing Components: Component Overview

Material	ET-F-WT500		Bicycle WT500											
Product. Plant	1200		Order start	01/29/2018										
Order Quantity	246	PC	Order finish	01/31/2018										

Component Overview

Material	Description	Requirement Qty	U...	C	Plant	Pr...	Supply Area	Reqmts date	V	Item	I.	Req...	B...	M.	I.
ET-1010	Bicycle frame CP	246	PC		1200			01/29/2018		0010	L	246		PC	PD
ET-1007	Pedal	492	PC		1200			01/29/2018		0020	L	492		PC	PD
ET-1005	Front wheel	246	PC		1200			01/29/2018		0030	L	246		PC	PD
ET-1006	Rear wheel	246	PC		1200			01/29/2018		0040	L	246		PC	PD
ET-1014	Gears CP	246	PC		1200			01/29/2018		0050	L	246		PC	PD
ET-1013	Chain	246	PC		1200			01/29/2018		0060	L	246		PC	ND

Figure 4.2: Displaying a planned order, component overview

4.3   Material requirements planning

Material planning takes place in SAP ERP using a program that is usually run every night. To keep the runtime of the program within acceptable limits (something which is necessary particularly in the case of a large number of materials), *net change planning* is used. It runs over the separate *planning file entry table* file. During the day, a flag is set for all materials for which planning-relevant changes take place. Consequently, during the nightly planning run, only those materials are planned that have a corresponding flag, and the flag is subsequently deleted. "Planning-relevant operations" include the recording of, or change to, a sales order; the creation of a DepReq (through the creation of a planned order), or a change to the planning parameters in the material master.

The second important value for executing material planning is the *low-level code*. This is assigned to every material and is updated as soon as it is used as a component in a bill of material. It describes the lowest level at which the material is integrated in all bill of material hierarchies. This information is required in the planning run so that all materials triggering requirements can be planned before the procurement proposals for the material are created.

For each material, the *gross requirements* are initially determined as part of the *requirements calculation*. In this calculation, the material quantities from planned independent requirements, customer orders, stock transfer orders, and/or dependent requirements are added together according to the material master settings.

The *stock calculation* is the counterpart to the requirements calculation. In the stock calculation, the applicable stock and permissible, previously-planned receipts are determined.

When we reconcile the results from the stock calculation and requirements calculation to one another, we get the net requirements, and therefore refer to *net requirements planning*. If only the gross requirements are used for planning, we refer to *gross requirements planning*.

In the *order quantity calculation*, where there is a deficit situation, the lot size settings from the material master are applied and a requirements coverage element created. This indicates the date on which the shortage should be compensated and with what quantity to be procured.

When the MRP run is started at night, a *net requirements calculation* is performed for every material, beginning with the first of the smallest low-level code. All requirements are subtracted from the warehouse stocks currently available, in chronological order, and all fixed stock receipts are added. This gives rise to a time series for the available quantities. If this value is negative, then there is a material *shortage* and new resources (= *planned order*) are created for this stock's deadline in the MRP run.

A planned order is an element that specifies when a specific quantity of the material is required to avoid a material shortage situation. It does not state whether the components required are already available or whether there is capacity available for manufacture. The quantity to be procured in the planned order is determined by the lot-sizing procedure entered in the material master and is added to the time series of available quantities. If there is still a shortage, planned orders are created until the shortage has been compensated.

Subsequently, in the MRP run, the other materials of this low-level code, and then the other low-level codes, are planned. The results of these net requirements calculations are saved in *MRP lists* so that the MRP controller responsible can follow the calculation if necessary. Using these lists, the controller can also identify and correct critical situations that have occurred in planning.

In our example, the sales department assumes that the new bicycle will be sold from January 2018 and has recorded planned requirement quantities according to target forecasts (see Figure 4.3).

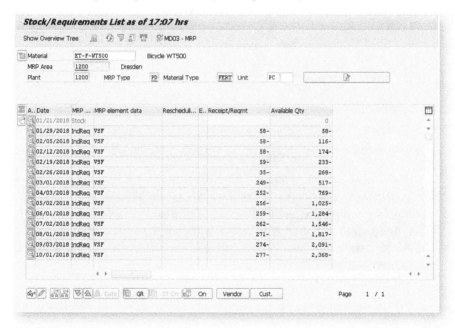

Figure 4.3: Stock/requirements list ET-F-WT500, independent requirements

The AVAILABLE QTY shows that a negative warehouse stock would cause a material shortage situation from July. In material requirements planning, SAP ERP now creates planned orders to cover the requirements in accordance with the lot-sizing procedure set. The exact lot size has been predefined for the bicycle; i.e., for each requirement element exactly one resource is created. Every planned order created (see Figure 4.4) generates dependent requirements for the components in accordance with its lead time and bill of material.

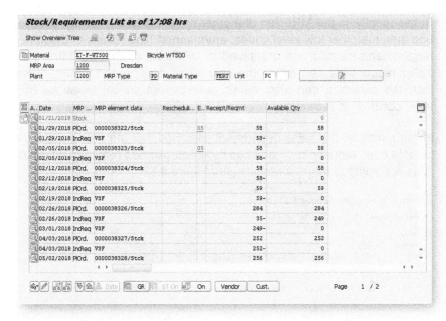

Stock/Requirements List as of 17:08 hrs

Show Overview Tree

Material	ET-F-WT500		Bicycle WT500			
MRP Area	1200	Dresden				
Plant	1200	MRP Type	PD	Material Type	FERT	Unit	PC

A..	Date	MRP ...	MRP element data	Rescheduli...	E..	Receipt/Reqmt	Available Qty
	01/21/2018	Stock					0
	01/29/2018	PlOrd.	0000038322/Stck	05		58	58
	01/29/2018	IndReq	VSF			58-	0
	02/05/2018	PlOrd.	0000038323/Stck	05		58	58
	02/05/2018	IndReq	VSF			58-	0
	02/12/2018	PlOrd.	0000038324/Stck			58	58
	02/12/2018	IndReq	VSF			58-	0
	02/19/2018	PlOrd.	0000038325/Stck			59	59
	02/19/2018	IndReq	VSF			59-	0
	02/26/2018	PlOrd.	0000038326/Stck			284	284
	02/26/2018	IndReq	VSF			35-	249
	03/01/2018	IndReq	VSF			249-	0
	04/03/2018	PlOrd.	0000038327/Stck			252	252
	04/03/2018	IndReq	VSF			252-	0
	05/02/2018	PlOrd.	0000038328/Stck			256	256

Date | GR | ST On | On | Vendor | Cust. | | Page 1 / 2

Figure 4.4: Stock/requirements list ET-F-WT500, with planned orders

I will now present one of these components in more detail. As seen in the STOCK/REQUIREMENTS LIST in Figure 4.5, the warehouse stock available for the rear wheel (material ET-1006) is 200 units in mid-January 2018. The dependent requirements are deducted from this quantity (each week) to determine the quantity still available. As you can see in this illustration, a material shortage does not occur until February 14.

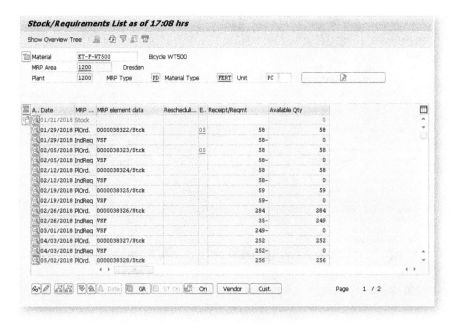

Figure 4.5: Stock/requirements list ET-1006, dependent requirements

The rear wheel is planned with a fixed lot size, because an acceptance of precisely 1000 units has been agreed with the supplier. Material requirements planning therefore creates a planned order with the corresponding quantity for every material shortage. As you can see in Figure 4.6, this ensures that there is always a certain residual quantity in the warehouse.

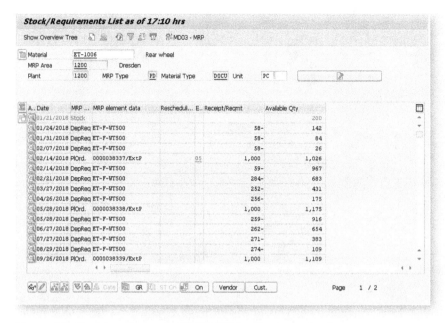

Figure 4.6: Stock/requirements list ET-1006, with planned orders

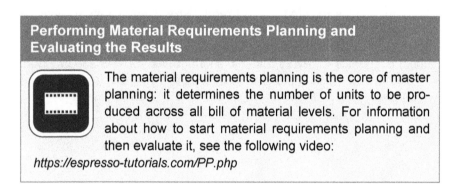

4.4 Evaluations

As mentioned in Section 4.3, an image of the stock/requirements situation is created for every planned material after the material requirements planning run—the *MRP list*. To display this for our bicycle planning, you can use transactions MD05 or MD06. It makes more sense to use the collective access to the data via transaction MD06 so that you can see all of the materials for the bicycle at a glance. Call up the transaction and enter MRP CONTROLLER 000 and PLANT 1200. You can then add further filter criteria to make the search results more precise. This allows you to exclude items that have been planned on a consumption-driven basis by limiting the selection to MRP type PD. Click 🖫 to save your selection criteria as a default setting. Figure 4.7 illustrates the example access to the transaction. You confirm the selection with the [Enter] key.

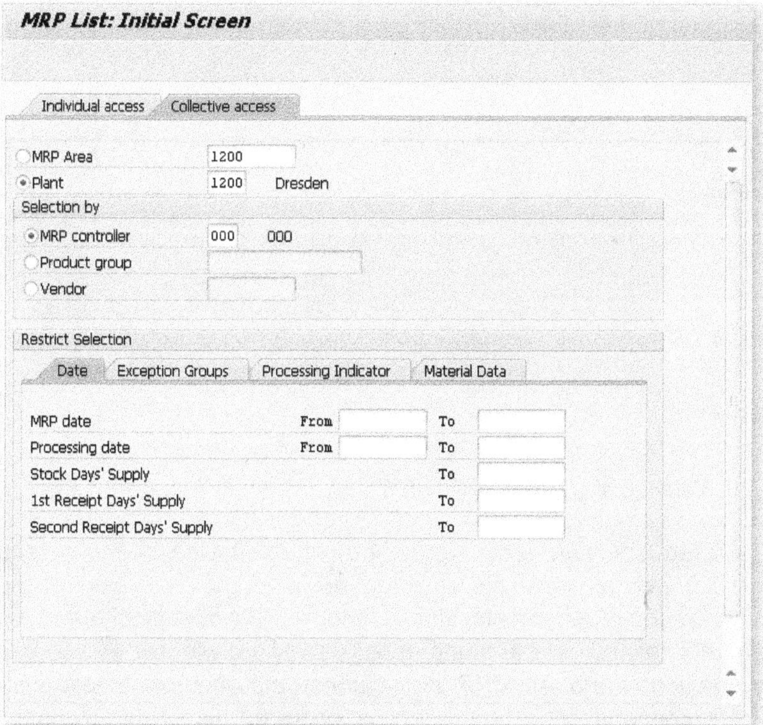

MRP List: Initial Screen

| Individual access | Collective access |

○ MRP Area   1200
● Plant   1200   Dresden

Selection by
● MRP controller   000   000
○ Product group
○ Vendor

Restrict Selection

| Date | Exception Groups | Processing Indicator | Material Data |

	From	To
MRP date	From	To
Processing date	From	To
Stock Days' Supply		To
1st Receipt Days' Supply		To
Second Receipt Days' Supply		To

Figure 4.7: Access to transaction MD06

In the window that opens, you see a list of all MRP lists that meet the selection criteria entered. You can sort this table and search in it to make it easier to select the materials for which you want to display the MRP lists. To do this, in the EDIT menu, select the SEARCH function to access the search screen. Alternatively, you can press the keyboard combination [Ctrl] + [F]. For example, you can search for specific MRP elements. After you run the search, the materials that meet the search criteria are highlighted in the table. If you want to display the MRP lists for the highlighted items, click SELECTED MRP LISTS (see Figure 4.8).

MRP List:: Material List

&y Selected MRP Lists   Define Traffic Light   ⓘ Exception Groups

| Plant | 1200 | Dresden |
| MRP Controller | 000 | 000 |

Light	Material	MRP Area	Material Description	CI	N1	2	3	4	5	6	7	8	StckDS	1st R...	2nd R	MRP date	Plan...	B...
☒◯◯	ET-2001	1200	aluminium tube D30 x 80		✓			4		2			444.5-	444.5-	444.5-	01/21/2018	200 PC	
☒◯◯	ET-2011	1200	lacquer: primer		✓			4		1			442.0-	442.0-	442.0-	01/21/2018	50 L	
◯◯☐	ET-1005	1200	Front wheel		✓ 2			8		2			2.0	2.0	2.0	01/21/2018	0 PC	
◯◯☐	ET-1006	1200	Rear wheel		✓ 1			2					17.4	17.4	17.4	01/21/2018	200 PC	
◯◯☐	ET-1007	1200	Pedal		✓ 2			10					2.0	2.0	2.0	01/21/2018	0 PC	
◯◯☐	ET-1010	1200	Bicycle frame CP		✓ 2			10					2.0	2.0	2.0	01/21/2018	0 PC	
◯◯☐	ET-1012	1200	Fork		✓			5		3			44.3	44.3	44.3	01/21/2018	600 PC	
◯◯☐	ET-1014	1200	Gears CP		✓			2		1			2.0	2.0	2.0	01/21/2018	0 PC	
◯◯☐	ET-2002	1200	aluminium tube D20 x 40										999.9	999.9	999.9	01/21/2018	0 PC	
◯◯☐	ET-2012	1200	lacquer: royal blue		✓			4					67.7	67.7	67.7	01/21/2018	550 L	
◯◯☐	ET-F-WT500	1200	Bicycle WT500		✓ 2			10					5.0	5.0	5.0	01/21/2018	0 PC	

Figure 4.8: Material list in transaction MD06

In the subsequent view (see Figure 4.9), the left side of the screen shows a list with all materials selected ❶, and the main part of the screen shows the requirements, stocks, and receipts directly after the net requirements calculation ❷. In the upper part of the window ❸ you can display additional data. An MRP list includes data about materials planning and exceptional situations that have occurred during this planning, as well as data from the planning views of the material master record and consumption data from recent months.

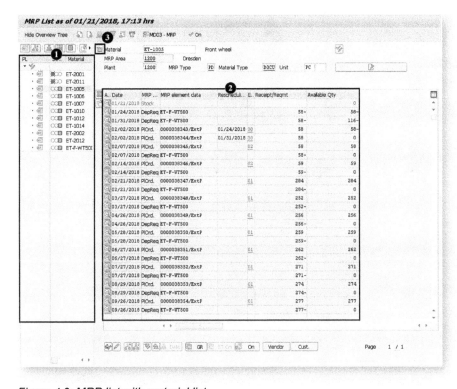

Figure 4.9: MRP list with material list

You can adjust this view to your own requirements. Via the menu path: ENVIRONMENT • OWN FAVORITES • MAINTAIN, you have access to a configuration menu (see Figure 4.10), in which you can create frequently required transactions as *Favorites*. These then appear in the function bar below the menu functions. All you have to do is select the transaction code, an icon, and the text, and then save the view.

User Settings for Flexible Transaction Calls

User Name	WEBER
Navigation no.	1

[i] Examples

Transaction code	MD03
☐ With initial screen	

Texts and Icon for Menu and Pushbutton

Text in Menu	MRP
Icon	ICON_OPERATION
Text for Icon	MD03 - MRP
Info text	

Preview Button: MD03 - MRP

Prepopulate Parameters for Initial Screen of Transaction

Parameter ID 1	MATNR	ParaValue1	
Parameter ID 2		ParValue 2	
Parameter ID 3		ParameterVal 3	

Offer Transaction Only If Defined in Material Master...

Proc. Type	
Material type	
MRP group	
MRP type	

Application	Only in operational planning (MD04, MD05, MD... ▼

Figure 4.10: Creating your own favorites

If you need more detailed information about the material situation for a specific order, select the order and activate the button next to the plant stock (see ❶ in Figure 4.11). Instead of the material list, you now see an order report ❷. This report shows the bill of material with the requirements date for the selected order, as well as the elements that cover this requirement. These can be stocks or other receipt elements such as planned orders or purchase requisitions. These displays also show whether supplying the order leads to exception messages for the components.

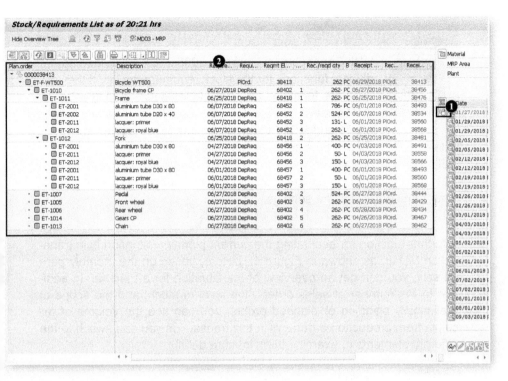

Figure 4.11: Order report in transaction MD06

With regard to the layout and functions, the MRP and the require-
ments/stock lists are similar. It is only the data displayed that is different.
Therefore, the information presented for access to the transaction, for
the overview table in the collective access, and for the actual list applies
equally for transactions MD04 and MD07 (Current Stock/Requirements
List). The difference is that transaction MD04 always shows the current
situation, and this may have changed since the materials planning.
Therefore, if you have made changes to the planning for an item during
the working day and want to analyze the effects, you should use transaction MD04.

Stock/requirements list for multiple materials

 With Enhancement Package 2005.2, SAP provided additional functions for the stock/requirements list. If the business function LOG_PP_LMAN is activated in your SAP system, you will see additional tabs in transactions MD04 and MD07 that you can use to call up consolidated lists. This can be a cross-plant display of the planning situation of a material or an overview of the planning situation for all materials of a product group in a plant. You can adjust this function to meet your requirements in the settings.

A further function for evaluating the current planning situation is in transaction MD48, as shown in Figure 4.12. Here, based on the monthly period split, you can get an overview of the situation for a material. In addition to the number of sales orders, the level of stock, and the scope of preliminary planning or planned orders, you can see the volume of receipts from production orders. With this transaction you can switch to the different elements to examine them in more detail.

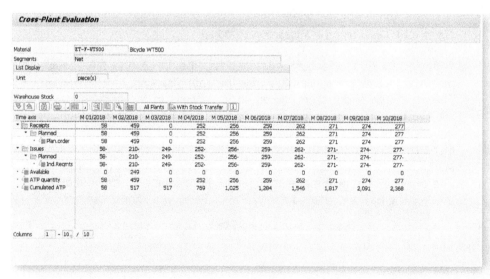

Figure 4.12: Planning overview MD48

The last transaction reflects the transition to Shop Floor Control. With transaction CO41 COLLECTIVE CONVERSION, you can select all planned orders, based on an opening date, and convert them into production orders in mass processing. This is by far the easiest way to create these orders. Once you have called up the transaction, select MRP Controller *000* and enter the current date as the latest creation date. The subsequent list (see Figure 4.13) contains all planned orders whose opening date has either been reached or already exceeded. By clicking the corresponding buttons, select all orders ❶ and using the CONVERT ❷ function, convert them into production orders.

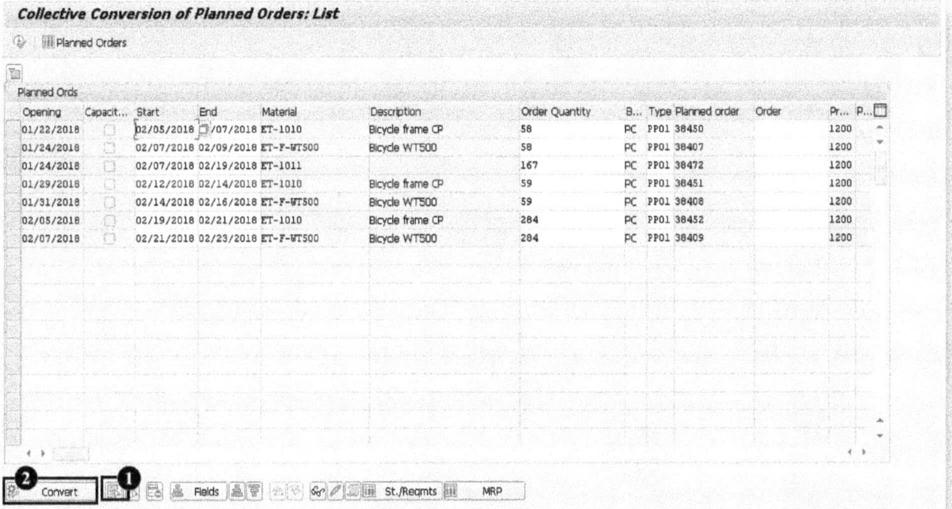

Figure 4.13: Collective conversion of planned orders, CO41

4.5 Summary

In this chapter, I presented the most important aspects of requirements planning in SAP ERP. Based on the planned requirement quantities for sales and operations planning (see Chapter 3), we performed material requirements planning for the entire structure of our bicycle. You learned what effect the requirements have on materials planning and what the function of planned orders is. Finally, we analyzed the materials planning results with different tools and we created production orders. The next chapter provides more detailed information on these elements and explains how you can use them to control and map production.

5 Shop floor control

For the planned production to be optimally executed and monitored, production orders have to be created. Below, I explain how these are set up and how you can work with them effectively.

5.1 Production order

Production orders are independent elements of Shop Floor Control. They are used to represent the production run, to print production papers, to document the degree of processing, to record material withdrawals, and to post the production activity required for manufacture. You can see that the order has an important role for control. Therefore, I will firstly outline basic principles for setting up a production order.

Just like a material master, for example, a production order consists of different layers (see Section 2.1. It unites the routing and bill of material master data with the header data. To prevent every change in Shop Floor Control causing an immediate adjustment to the master data, when you create a production order, a copy of the routing and the bill of material is created especially for this order (see Figure 5.1). You can create production orders from a planned order (see Section 4.4) or manually with transaction CO01 (SAP MENU • LOGISTICS • PRODUCTION • SHOP FLOOR CONTROL • ORDER • CREATE). You process the production orders created with transaction CO02.

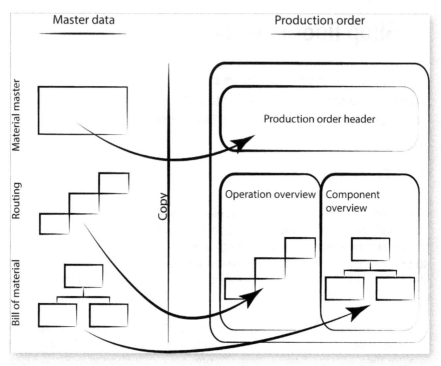

Figure 5.1: Master data interaction for a production order

The initial screen of a production order usually shows the header data. Here, we use the example of a bicycle fork, as shown in Figure 5.2. In particular, this data unites organizational details and control parameters for the planned order processing. For example, basic dates are displayed, as well as the execution dates from the first to the last activity and the release date. These are then compared to the actual dates. Further tabs contain, in particular, control parameters, including parameters for goods movements, costing, and scheduling. The MRP controller key is also defined here, as well as the bill of material and the routing used. The header area of the screen contains basic data such as the order number, material, plant, and order type. Below the header data the scheduling type applied and the float (buffer) times considered are displayed.

Here you can call up a list of the total and scrap quantities and the number of pieces already delivered.

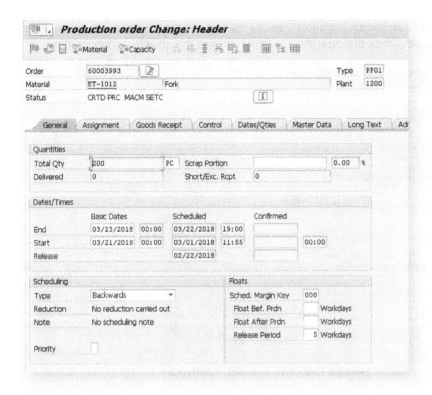

Figure 5.2: Order header data, fork production order

You can see the routing that is the basis for the order execution under the OPERATION OVERVIEW (see Figure 5.3). Here, the data from the standard routing (see Section 2.4) has been supplemented with the dates for the lead time scheduling. Every operation of an order has a status and an individual completion confirmation number that can be used to confirm an activity or quantity.

Personalizing the column arrangement

 You can adapt this overview, just like many others, to meet your own requirements by shifting the column (headers) with the mouse and then saving the arrangement as a template. To do this, click the symbol to the right of the column headers.

You can switch from this view to the view of the operation details – either double-click the operation number or click the corresponding button.

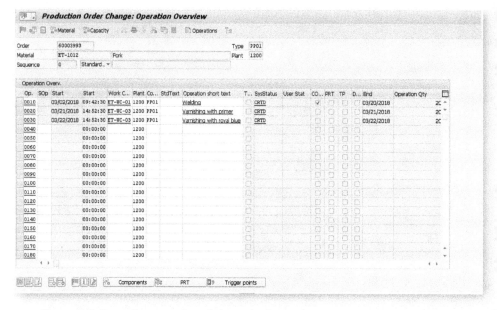

Figure 5.3: Operation overview, fork production order

The bill of material for the order is also copied and supplemented with further data. As soon as you have assigned individual parts to an operation, the individual requirements date for each component is transferred from the operation—provided the system is configured in this way. This assignment therefore has the effect of shifting the requirements date of the component from the basic start date to the start date of the respective operation. The order BOM documents, for example, for each individual component, whether and how much of this material has already been withdrawn (see Figure 5.4).

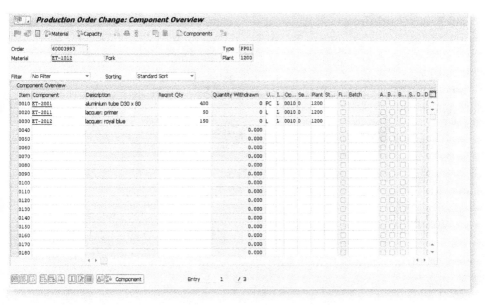

Figure 5.4: Component overview, fork production order

The easiest way to switch between these views is by clicking the buttons in the order's toolbar (see Figure 5.5). You can also see the most important functions for processing the order; for example, for releasing or scheduling it.

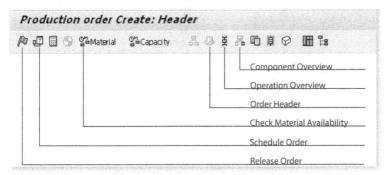

Figure 5.5: Toolbar in the production order

5.2 Scheduling

One of the most important functions of the production order is *lead time scheduling*. Depending on the setting, scheduling is either forwards from the basic start date of the planned order or backwards from the *basic finish* date.

Forwards/backwards scheduling

 The decision whether to schedule forwards or backwards depends on the MRP procedure used.

If you use planning-driven or requirements-driven materials planning, you calculate backwards from the requirement. In contrast, if you use reorder point materials planning, then when you create the order, you calculate forwards from the date of creation.

SAP ERP receives the data required for scheduling from the copied routing, the related work centers, and the *scheduling margin key* transferred from the material master to the header data.

A production order consists of a number of different dates and scheduling parameters. I will present the most important values based on Figure 5.6.

Every order covers two basic dates that position the order relative to other orders. The basic start date defines the requirement date for the components and the basic finish date defines when production is complete. Both dates are always created on a day basis; i.e., not for a specific time.

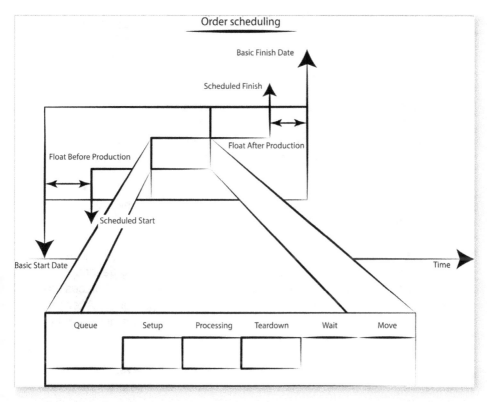

Figure 5.6: Order and operation scheduling

The scheduled start and finish dates of the order represent dates for production operations and are separated from the basic dates by time buffers (referred to as "floats"). The *scheduled finish* is the completion time of the last operation of the order and is separated from the *basic finish* date by the *float after production*. The start of the first operation is also the *scheduled start* and follows the *basic start* date by the *float before production*. These dates are created taking the availability of the required work center into account, and they stipulate a time (see again Figure 5.2).

The production operations take place one after the other between the two dates. Each of these operations consists of different sections that are all planned to the precise minute; the *queue time* specifies the required time from the "arrival" of an order at the work center to the start of setup. As this float is a mean value, it is not clear whether in an individual case it is as large as assumed. Therefore, the entry of a queue time means that in ERP, both an earliest (without queue time) and a latest (with full queue time) point of execution (of work) are created for every operation. The order is then executed between these two extreme points.

Setup, *processing*, and *tear down* are the sections in which work takes place at the work center. During setup, the work center/machine is prepared for the order; for example, tools are provided, test equipment is organized, and the machine program is loaded. The setup time is not dependent on the number of units in the order. Processing describes the period in which—as the name already indicates—the workpieces are processed. It is dependent on the number of units produced. After processing, the machine is stripped down and cleaned. The time required for this is also not dependent on the number of units.

If there are special technological features that prevent immediate transport of the goods to the next work center (e.g., time for hardened goods to cool down or for painted parts to dry), this is a (process-related) *queue time*. The last section of an operation is the *transport time* to the next operation.

Let us take a more detailed look at scheduling using an order for the production of the bicycle fork. Backwards scheduling is set for this order; the same relationships and dependencies apply for the forwards calculation, but in the reverse order. The result of the net requirements calculation was that the production order must be completed on *03/23/2018*. This is the basic finish date, which results from Figure 5.2 and, as an extract of the order header, also from Figure 5.7 (see ❶).

Because there is no float after production built into the scheduling margin key ❷, the scheduled end is connected to the *basic finish* date ❸. In our example, this is *03/22/2018* at *19:00*. This date is also the last date of operation 0030 ❹, the third and final production step in this order. Before the tear down, process, and setup operations are scheduled, a required wait time of *120 minutes* must be deducted starting from this date. This means that the painter must set up or prepare his work center for this order by *03/22/2018, 14:52* at the latest. Before setup, the wait time (here, six hours) is included in the calculation. This results in an earliest possible point of execution for the operation that is exactly zero hours offset to the latest point of execution. Therefore, the operation can finish at the earliest on *03/22/2018* at *12:37*, and must therefore be set up on *03/22/2018* by *08:30*. The previous operation—0020 (painting with base coat)—is aligned with this earliest possible point of execution for the setup. This scheduling loop is repeated for every operation.

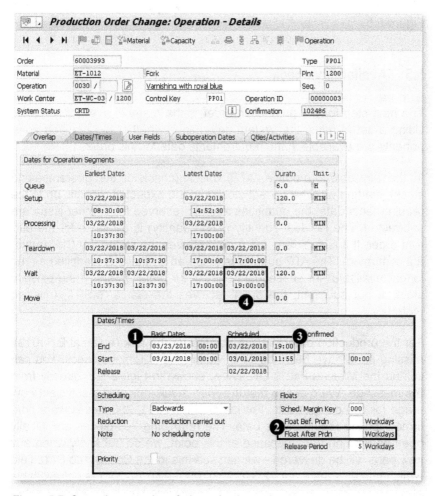

Figure 5.7: Operation overview, fork production order

97

The earliest possible deadline for the setup in operation 0010 (welding) determines the scheduled start that you see in the order header. The release date for the order is thus *five working days* (the number of days specified in the RELEASE PERIOD field) before the scheduled start. It is a control date for the release of the production orders, similar to the opening date for the planned orders.

A production order is scheduled automatically when it is created and when it is saved. If changes occur in the meantime and you want to reschedule the order, you can do this by clicking the relevant symbol (see Figure 5.5).

5.3 Availability check

The next step for the production order is the *material availability check*. Using a set of rules, the system determines whether the required components are available at the requirements date for this order.

In the *available-to-promise (ATP) check* (check of the guaranteeable stock), starting with the current stock and the expected receipts up to the requirements date, the quantities already reserved for another issue are subtracted. The residual quantity (ATP quantity) is available for the current order. If it is sufficient, the order receives the status "MACM" (material confirmed). The ATP quantity is reserved so that it is identified as "no longer available" for subsequent checks for other orders. If the existing stock is not sufficient, the order receives the status "MSPT" (missing material).

For the production order that we created for the fork (material ET-1012), missing parts have been identified during the automatic check. You can call up the MISSING PARTS OVERVIEW, shown in Figure 5.8, directly from the message. We can see that the ATP check indicated insufficient coverage for two components. For material ET-2001, 200 pieces were confirmed for the requirements date. The remaining 200 pieces are initially open as missing parts because at this point, we do not know when any new parts will be delivered—we can see this in the COMMITTED DATE field (which contains the entry *12/31/9999*). MATERIAL *ET-2011* is not available at all on the requirements date, but the system has been able to determine that on *04/03/2018*, the entire *50 L* will be available and therefore, in this line the committed date was set to that date.

Production Order Change: Missing Parts Overview

Order 60003993   Type PP01
Material ET-1012   Fork   Plant 1200

Total Commitment Date 04/25/2018

Overview Missing Parts

Item Material	Requireme...	Requirement Quantity	Confirmed quantity	B...	Committe...	Ac...	St...	Material Description	Batch	ATP qu...
0010 ET-2001	03/01/2018	400	200	PC	12/31/9999	0010		aluminium tube D30 x ..		
0020 ET-2011	03/01/2018	50	0	L	04/03/2018	0010		lacquer: primer		
0040		0.000	0.000							
0050		0.000	0.000							
0060		0.000	0.000							
0070		0.000	0.000							
0080		0.000	0.000							
0090		0.000	0.000							
0100		0.000	0.000							
0110		0.000	0.000							
0120		0.000	0.000							
0130		0.000	0.000							
0140		0.000	0.000							
0150		0.000	0.000							
0160		0.000	0.000							
0170		0.000	0.000							
0180		0.000	0.000							
0190		0.000	0.000							
0200		0.000	0.000							
0210		0.000	0.000							
0220		0.000	0.000							
0230		0.000	0.000							
0240		0.000	0.000							
0250		0.000	0.000							

Component   Entry   1   / 2

Figure 5.8: Missing parts overview, fork production

At this point, we are interested in how material ET-2011 is confirmed and we check this component in detail again. To do this, we select the line and click [Component]. A confirmation proposal is displayed (see Figure 5.9). In this proposal, we cannot see yet how the result arose. In the check result, however, we see again that confirmation on the requested delivery date is not possible; complete confirmation can only take place on 04/03/2018, and there is only one—the complete—confirmation proposal. If the SAP system could propose partial confirmations, these would be displayed in this section, but this is not the case in our example. To see the detailed information that the check was based on, in a subsequent view, we click ATP QUANTITIES.

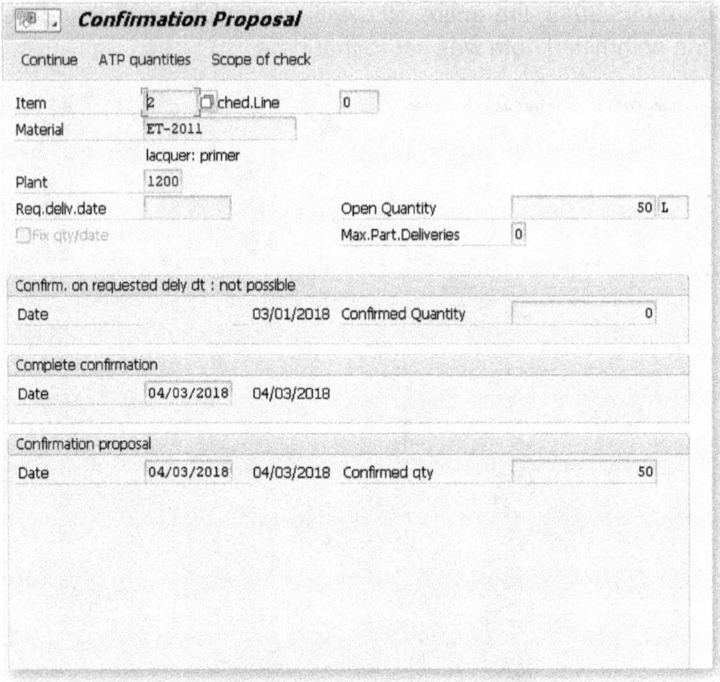

Figure 5.9: Confirmation proposal, paint—base coat

The AVAILABILITY OVERVIEW that now opens shows, in the ATP SITUATION area, how the results of the check arose (see Figure 5.10). The receipts/required quantities for the relevant MRP elements are presented in chronological order. We already know this form from the stock/requirements list (see Section 4.3); here, however, the CONFIRMED and CUM. ATP QTY columns have been added. (CUM. ATP QTY indicates the total quantity available at this point)

We see that the warehouse stock (STOCK) of *50 L* has already been confirmed for an order allocation in February; this means, however, that it is no longer available for our current check (represented by the MRP element SIMREQ) for *03/01/2018*. The next receipt does not take place until *04/03/2018* and supplies a quantity of *178 L* due to a planned order (PIORD). This goods receipt led to the confirmation date that was visible on the previous screen.

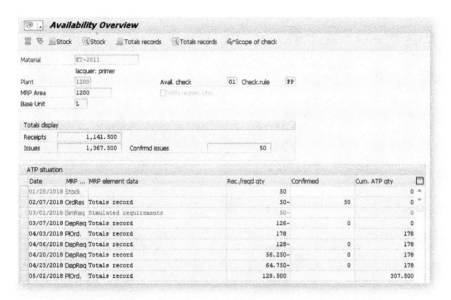

Figure 5.10: Availability overview, paint: base coat

5.4 Order release

Production should take place as soon as planning and order creation are complete. The *order release* is the trigger. The following activities can only take place once this has happened:

▶ printing of shop floor papers

▶ posting of stock withdrawals

▶ confirmation of operations

▶ posting of stock receipts (into warehouse/stores)

You can execute the release interactively in the order by clicking the corresponding button in the order header ❶ (see Figure 5.11). You see immediately how the STATUS ❷ changes from CRTD (created) to REL (released). All remaining open activities linked to the release (e.g., automatic printing) are executed when you save the order ❸.

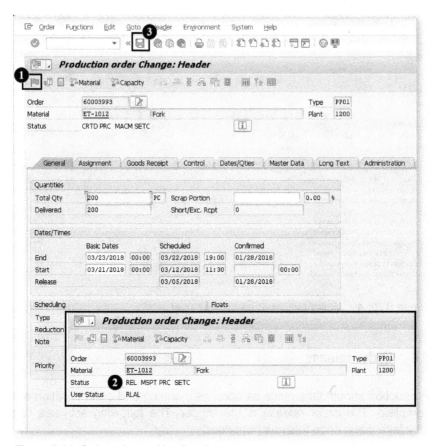

Figure 5.11: Order release, Header view

Alternatively, you can execute a mass release via transaction CO05N: SAP MENU • LOGISTICS • PRODUCTION • SHOP FLOOR CONTROL• CONTROL (for the initial screen, see Figure 5.12). Restricting the selection is particularly helpful here. You can restrict it based on the value in the SCHEDULED RELEASE DATE, in field ❶. This ensures that only those orders that should be released from a scheduling perspective are selected. The restriction to our bicycle parts is via the production plant *1200* and the MRP controller *000* ❷. You can refine the selection further via the system status ❸ and, for example, select only those orders that no longer contain missing parts. You start the transaction by pressing F8 or by clicking ⬦.

Release Production Orders

⊕ ⊡ ⊡

List	Order Headers ▼
Layout	000000000001 Standard Layout

| Selection | Mass Processing - Release |

Select. at Header Level

Production Order		to		⇪
Material		to		⇪
Production Plant	1200	to		⇪
Planning plant	❷	to		⇪
Order Type		to		⇪
MRP Controller	000	to		⇪
Prodn Supervisor		to		⇪
Sold-To Party		to		⇪
Sales Order		to		⇪
Sales Order Item		to		⇪
WBS Element		to		⇪
Sequence number		to		⇪
Priority		to		⇪
Status Selection Profile				
Syst. Status	☐ Excl. ❸ and ☐ Excl.			
Stock Segment		to		⇪

Absolute Dates at Header Level

Basic Start Date		to		⇪
Basic Finish Date		to		⇪
Scheduled Start Date		to		⇪
Scheduled Finish Date		to		⇪
Scheduled Release Date		to	01/31/2018 ❶	⇪
Actual Start Date		to		⇪
Actual Finish Date		to		⇪
Actual Release Date		to		⇪

Figure 5.12: Initial screen of the mass release of production orders, CO05N

The subsequent order list shows the orders that match our selection (see Figure 5.13). If everything is OK and we want to release all of these orders, we select them all by clicking the corresponding button ❶ and then start the release by clicking the MASS PROCESSING button ❷.

Figure 5.13: Execution of mass release of production orders

5.5 Material withdrawal

Once the order has been released, the components must be withdrawn from the warehouse. We post this withdrawal with transaction MIGO: SAP MENU • LOGISTICS • MATERIALS MANAGEMENT • INVENTORY MANAGEMENT • GOODS MOVEMENT, with reference to the production order (see Figure 5.14). From the dropdown menu, we select the *Goods Issue* and *Order* options ❶, and in the third field, enter our order number *60003993*. SAP ERP has already derived the correct movement type *261* GI FOR ORDER from our selection ❷ and displays this. We confirm the entry of the order number by pressing ⌊Enter⌋ and the components of this order are now displayed.

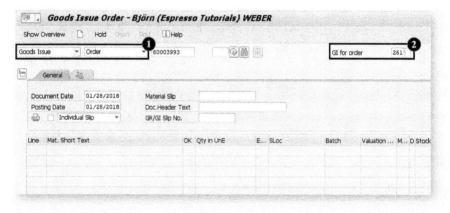

Figure 5.14: Recording the goods issue with transaction MIGO, initial screen

For each component of the production order, we can now adjust the quantity and the storage location (see Figure 5.15). If we are happy with the values entered, we select the items we want to post by placing a checkmark in the OK field and then click POST.

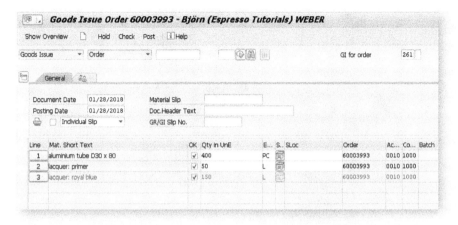

Figure 5.15: Recording the goods issue, selecting the components

The posting has several effects:

▶ The stock is reduced.

▶ The requirements are reduced.

▶ The actual costs are debited to the order.

▶ A material document and an accounting document are created to document the movement of goods.

You can also track the result of the posting in the COMPONENT OVERVIEW of the production order (see Figure 5.16). In the corresponding columns you can see the QUANTITY WITHDRAWN ❶ and an indicator that states whether the item was withdrawn completely ❷.

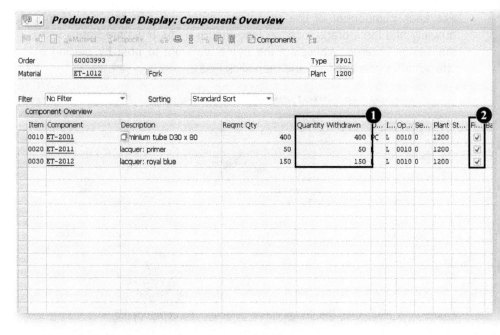

Figure 5.16: Production order, components withdrawn

If certain regularly required components, such as screws, are not in the warehouse but are held in stock in the assembly work center, a material withdrawal by means of backflushing is more useful than a posting in the warehouse.

Backflushing

In backflushing, the posting of the material is connected to the confirmation of the operation. When you confirm an operation to which materials are assigned in the component assignment (see Section 2.4), and these materials are identified as BACKFLUSHING, a material withdrawal for the quantity in the confirmation quantity that you entered is executed.

5.6   Confirmations

You use *Confirmation* to record production progress and make it transparent for other users of the ERP system. This enables you to monitor your production and to intervene to make corrections when necessary. You can enter the following values in the confirmation:

- ▶ quantities
- ▶ activities
- ▶ deadlines
- ▶ HR data
- ▶ work centers

The backflushing already showed that a confirmation covers more than just the documentation of quantities and activities. For example, further actual costs are debited to the production order based on the activities reported. The confirmation can also trigger an automatic goods receipt posting for the order, and this posting offsets a backflushing.

The most common form of confirmation is the *time ticket*, which you can confirm using transaction CO11N (see Figure 5.17). After ending an operation, start the transaction and in the CONFIRMATION field ❶, enter the confirmation number of the operation. After you press the ⌜Enter⌟ key the ERP system loads the order data and you can edit the good and scrap quantity ❷ if necessary, as well as the required activity (setup, machine, and labor ratios) ❸. The confirmation is executed as soon as you save by clicking the disk icon ❹.

Partial confirmations

 You do not always have to confirm the entire operation with the complete number of units. You can also execute a partial confirmation of quantity and activity at the end of a shift or working day. This documents the current degree of processing and is traceable for other SAP users.

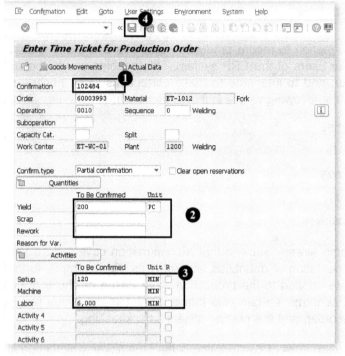

Figure 5.17: Recording confirmation, CO11N

5.7 Goods receipts for production orders

In Section 5.5, we recorded the goods issue for the components. We now have to post the goods receipt for the finished material when it arrives in the warehouse.

To do this, we start transaction MIGO again (see Figure 5.18). This time, however, we select the *Goods Receipt* and *Order* functions and add our order number again. The SAP ERP system again proposes the correct goods movement *101*.

Once we have confirmed the order number by pressing $\boxed{\text{Enter}}$, the first line displays the target material of our production order with the order quantity (see Figure 5.19). In the item details, we can review all the data before clicking POST to post the goods movement.

Figure 5.18: Recording the goods receipt, initial screen of transaction MIGO

Figure 5.19: Recording the goods receipt, completing transaction MIGO

This posting has the following effects:

▶ The material stock is increased.

▶ The open receipt quantity for the production order is reduced.

▶ The production order is credited with the actual costs, and a material document and an accounting document are created to document the goods movement.

We call up the production order with transaction CO03 to check it and in Figure 5.20, we can now see that the production order shows a delivered quantity of *200 pieces*. This means that the entire planned quantity has now been delivered to the warehouse.

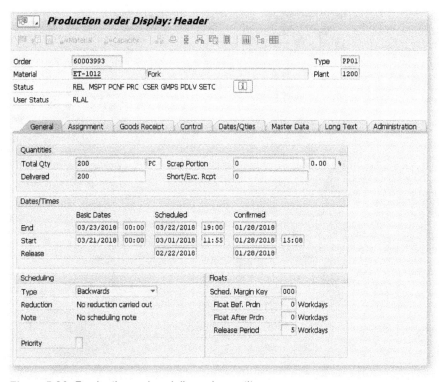

Figure 5.20: Production order, delivered quantity

6 Capacity requirements planning

The service to be provided for the production—the capacity requirement—always requires a free available capacity in order to be executed.

In this chapter, I show you how to get an overview of your capacity load utilization and how to plan effectively with limited capacities.

6.1 Capacity evaluations

A simple way of getting an overview of the utilization of your work centers and machines is to compare the capacity requirements of your orders and the existing available capacity of the work centers. In the SAP ERP system, transactions CM01 and CM02 (SAP MENU • LOGISTICS • PRODUCTION • CAPACITY PLANNING • EVALUATION • WORK CENTER VIEW) allow this type of evaluation.

The capacity requirements are calculated from the standard values and order quantity defined in the routing using the formula set in the work center. Note, however, that there are different formulas for scheduling and capacity calculation! The capacity requirements are usually reduced by the confirmation of the corresponding operation. The requirement is usually updated corresponding to the quantity confirmed.

The available capacity is maintained for each work center for every capacity category. To do this, enter the shift schedule of the work center in the master data of the work center capacity. If no shift schedule is maintained, you can also work with the standard available capacity. This is set approximately and constant for the future, meaning that no fluctuations (e.g., vacation) can be considered.

If you want to get an overview of the capacity load for a work center (e.g., for welding station ET-WC-01), use transaction CM01. For our example, on the initial screen, enter work center *ET-WC-01* and plant *1200* and confirm with the ⎡Enter⎤ key. The standard overview of the capacity load utilization appears. For each calendar week, you can see the total requirements from the production orders, the available capacity for the work center, and a resulting calculated percentage load. Weeks with a load exceeding 100% are highlighted red. In our example, as seen in Figure 6.1, the work center is overloaded in weeks 11 and 12.

If you want to know which orders led to this overload, you can select the required periods with a checkmark ❶ and then, by clicking CAP. DE-TAILS/PERIOD ❷, display a list of the individual orders.

Capacity Planning: Standard Overview

Cap. details/period ❷

| Work center | ET-WC-01 | Welding | | | Plant | 1200 |
| Capacity cat.: | 002 | Welding | | | | |

Week	Requirements	AvailCap.	CapLoad	RemAvailCap	Unit
04/2018	0.00	0.00	0 %	0.00	H
05/2018	0.00	80.00	0 %	80.00	H
06/2018	18.95	80.00	24 %	61.05	H
07/2018	37.22	80.00	47 %	42.78	H
08/2018	0.00	80.00	0 %	80.00	H
09/2018	0.00	80.00	0 %	80.00	H
10/2018	0.00	80.00	0 %	80.00	H
11/2018	89.00	80.00	111 %	9.00-	H
12/2018	97.50	80.00	122 %	17.50-	H
13/2018	0.00	64.00	0 %	64.00	H
Total >>>	242.67	704.00	35 %	461.33	H

Figure 6.1: Standard overview of the capacity load utilization CM01

This detailed capacity list is very similar to the list that appears when you call up transaction CM02. The difference to the transaction call is in the periods displayed (see Figure 6.2). If you navigate away from CM01, only the weeks you have selected are displayed.

In contrast, if you call up the capacity detail screen from transaction CM02, you can see all the coming weeks' requirements; in comparison to CM01, no available capacity is visible here. In the illustration, you can see that the capacity requirements of an order have been distributed to the individual weeks in accordance with the scheduling.

Capacity Planning: Standard Overview: Details

⬛ ⬛ ⬛ Order header   Choose fields...   Download

Plant   1200   Dresden
Work center   ET-WC-01   Welding
Capacity cat.   002   Labor

Week	P	PeggedRqmt	Material	PgRqmtQty	Reqmnts	Earl.start	LatestFin.
Total					186.50 H		
11/2018		60003993	ET-1012	200 PC	68.50 H	03/12/2018	03/21/2018
11/2018		60003997	ET-1011	252 PC	20.50 H	03/15/2018	03/22/2018
12/2018		60003993	ET-1012	200 PC	33.50 H	03/12/2018	03/21/2018
12/2018		60003997	ET-1011	252 PC	64.00 H	03/15/2018	03/22/2018

Figure 6.2: Capacity detail screen of the capacity load utilization CM01

6.2   Capacity leveling

In the previous section, you saw that at work center ET-WC-01, the load exceeded the available capacity in two calendar weeks; the work center is overloaded. During your daily work, you will encounter many such situations and each one will be slightly different. Therefore, there is no "one correct" solution for handling this situation or one form that capacity leveling should take. Therefore, in this section, I not only present a transaction but also show you some options for which you do not need a new SAP function. In principle, there are two approaches for reducing the load in the overloaded weeks:

▶   increase the available capacity, or

▶   reduce the capacity requirements.

You can generally increase the available capacity over the short term in two ways: you either use an additional individual capacity (however, this is only possible for work centers operated by personnel), or the available employees have to work longer (e.g., at the weekend).

If one of these options is available to you, in the SAP system, call up transaction CR12 to change the available capacity. On the initial screen, enter PLANT 1200, WORK CENTER ET-WC-01, and CAPACITY CATEGO-RY 002 and press the ⌈Enter⌋ key to confirm. The standard available capacity set appears on the subsequent screen (see Figure 6.3). Assuming that we have a third welder who can be deployed in the two weeks of the capacity overload, you have to increase the available capacity accordingly. To do this, we click the INTERVALS AND SHIFTS button ❶ to adjust the shift plan that applies to this work center.

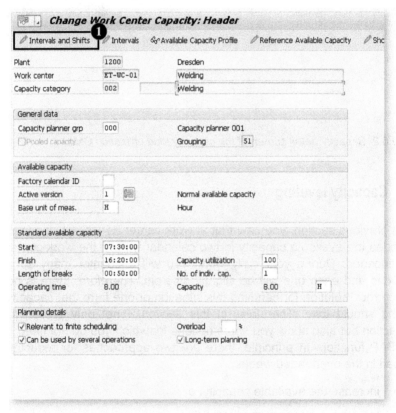

Figure 6.3: Changing the work center capacity, Header

The overview of the intervals of available capacity then appears (see Figure 6.4). In the lower area of the display ❶, you can see all intervals with the relevant valid shift plan. Here we can see that on this work center, work is performed on five days with two shifts each day: the early shift *F-11* and the late shift *S-11*. Originally, only one person was planned for each shift. However, to increase the available capacity, we enter *2* as the number of individual capacities in the early shift ❷. This means that on this work center, three employees work in two shifts.

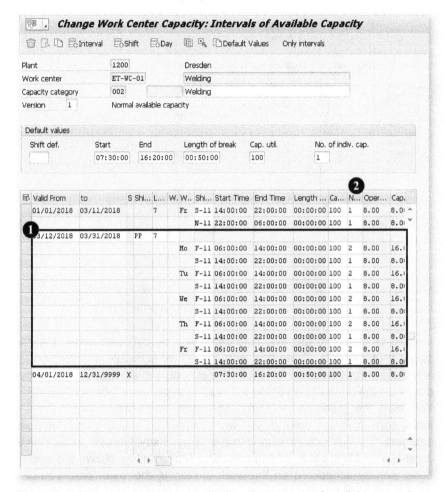

Figure 6.4: Changing the capacity, adjusting the intervals of available capacity

We check the result of our capacity increase by calling up transaction CM01 again (see Figure 6.5). We have eliminated the overload in CW11 and CW12. In fact, we have done more than that—there is now enough free capacity in production to process even more orders. The use of a third employee to increase the capacity therefore eliminates our bottleneck in production.

Capacity Planning: Standard Overview

🔳 🔁 Cap. details/period

| Work center | ET-WC-01 | Welding | Plant | 1200 |
| Capacity cat.: | 002 | Welding | | |

Week	Requirements	AvailCap.	CapLoad	RemAvailCap	Unit
04/2018	0.00	0.00	0 %	0.00	H
05/2018	0.00	80.00	0 %	80.00	H
06/2018	18.95	80.00	24 %	61.05	H
07/2018	37.22	80.00	47 %	42.78	H
08/2018	0.00	80.00	0 %	80.00	H
09/2018	0.00	80.00	0 %	80.00	H
10/2018	0.00	80.00	0 %	80.00	H
11/2018	89.00	120.00	74 %	31.00	H
12/2018	97.50	120.00	81 %	22.50	H
13/2018	0.00	96.00	0 %	96.00	H
Total >>>	242.67	816.00	30 %	573.33	H

Figure 6.5: Capacity requirements planning, Standard Overview

Instead of changing the available capacity, you can also adjust the capacity requirements. To do this, you can either schedule an order on an alternative work center or shift it in the schedule. I will explain the procedure with the latter option using the graphical planning table in SAP ERP. You start the *graphical planning table* with transaction CM21. On the initial screen, enter plant *1200*, work center *ET-WC-01*, and capacity category *002*. After confirming with the ⌈Enter⌋ key, we see an overview, as shown in Figure 6.6. The upper part of the window shows the operations already scheduled on the work center. In the lower part, you can see the pool of orders not yet scheduled. In our case, this list contains the orders for the frame and the fork. As explained in Section 6.1, the components for the fork will not arrive until later, which is why the operation had to be split. Therefore, we also schedule this order first.

To do so, click the OPERATION ❶ and then the SCHEDULE symbol (❷, alternatively, ⌈F5⌋). The bar for this operation is now in the scheduled operations area (see Figure 6.7 ❶).

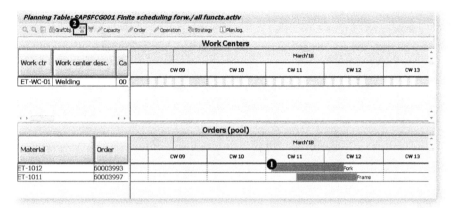

Figure 6.6: Graphical planning table, view before scheduling

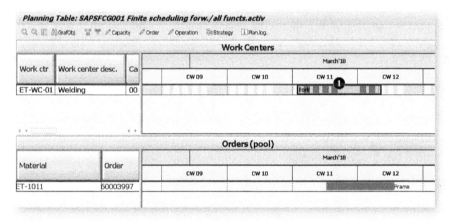

Figure 6.7: Graphical planning table, forks scheduled

As the forks currently occupy the two individual capacities of the work center, production of the bicycle frames is not possible in weeks 11 and 12. If you now schedule this operation, the SAP system shifts it automatically. In our example, the settings mean that the operation would be brought forward to produce the frame before the fork. If you select the operation in the pool and click SCHEDULE, the operation is scheduled accordingly. In Figure 6.8 you can see that the order for the frame now has to start in week 10 because it has been brought forward. To save this sequence, simply click the disk symbol. The rescheduling is now saved.

117

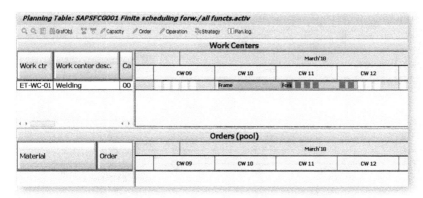

Figure 6.8: Graphical planning table, bicycle frames and forks scheduled

To check whether the overload situation has actually been resolved, call up transaction CM01 again. In Figure 6.9, you can see that this procedure has eliminated the capacity overload. However, you have to check separately whether all required components will be available for this earlier deadline (see Section 5.3).

Capacity Planning: Standard Overview

🔲 🔄 Cap. details/period

Work center   ET-WC-01   Welding   Plant   1200
Capacity cat.: 002   Welding

Week	Requirements	AvailCap.	CapLoad	RemAvailCap	Unit
04/2018	0.00	0.00	0 %	0.00	H
05/2018	0.00	80.00	0 %	80.00	H
06/2018	18.95	80.00	24 %	61.05	H
07/2018	37.22	80.00	47 %	42.78	H
08/2018	0.00	80.00	0 %	80.00	H
09/2018	0.00	80.00	0 %	80.00	H
10/2018	75.30	80.00	94 %	4.70	H
11/2018	77.70	80.00	97 %	2.30	H
12/2018	33.50	80.00	42 %	46.50	H
13/2018	0.00	64.00	0 %	64.00	H
Total >>>	242.67	704.00	35 %	461.33	H

Figure 6.9: Capacity requirements planning, standard overview

7 Summary

For manufacturing companies, production planning is *the* central process; a production company can only sustainably achieve its objectives if this process is effectively and efficiently mapped. This makes the PP module extremely relevant for SAP customers in this area. In writing this book, my aim was to clearly explain the underlying planning approach and its methodology. I covered the master data involved in planning processes and how it is structured. Using our bicycle example, we traced the sales and operations planning and the material requirements planning, and their process flow. I showed you the importance of production orders for lot-related production and which functions they perform. Finally, you learned how to implement capacity sequencing using capacity leveling in SAP ERP.

I hope that this book has provided you with an informative overview of production planning in SAP ERP. While reading this book, you will certainly have become aware that planning processes are much more detailed than can be presented as part of an introduction. You could easily fill an entire book for each chapter.

I imagine you decided to read this book because you were looking for a quick introduction and overview of SAP PP. If you want to look deeper into this topic, I recommend that you try things out in practice. Remain inquisitive! If you are a student, you can ask at your college or university whether they have access to an IDES (International Demonstration and Education System). If you are an employee, then ask at work about access to an IDES or test system. Additionally, in every SAP system, you can use the F1 key to get quick and uncomplicated access to help/documentation. Alternatively, you can use the SAP online help at any time under *http://help.sap.com*. However you proceed, I hope that the basic knowledge I have provided in this book has given you a good basis for looking at, and dealing with, the topic of production planning in more detail.

A Transaction Overview

CA01	Create Routing
CA02	Change Routing
CA03	Display Routing
CM01	Capacity Planning, Work Center Load
CM02	Capacity Planning, Work Center Orders
CM21	Capacity Leveling: SFC Planning Table
CO01	Create Production Order
CO02	Change Production Order
CO03	Display Production Order
CO05N	Collective Release Production Order
CO11N	Enter Time Ticket
CO41	Collective Conversion of Planned Orders
CR01	Create Work Center
CR02	Change Work Center
CR03	Display Work Center
MC35	Create Rough-Cut Planning Profile
MC36	Change Rough-Cut Planning Profile
MC37	Display Rough-Cut Planning Profile
MC75	Transfer PG to Demand Management
MC81	Create Planning for Product Group
MC82	Change Planning for Product Group
MC83	Display Planning for Product Group
MC84	Create Product Group
MC85	Display Product Group
MC86	Change Product Group

CR12	Change Capacity
CR13	Display Capacity
CS01	Create Material BOM
CS02	Change Material BOM
CS03	Display Material BOM
MD04	Stock/Requirements List
MD05	MRP List (individual access)
MD06	MRP List (collective access)
MD07	Current Material Overview
MD44	MPS Evaluation
MD48	Planning Situation: All Plants
MD61	Create Planned Independent Requirements
MD62	Change Planned Independent Requirements
MD63	Display Planned Independent Requirements
MD67	Staggered Split
MIGO	Goods Movement (MIGO)
MM01	Create Material (immediately)
MM02	Change Material (immediately)
MM03	Display Material (current status)

You have finished the book.

B The Author

Björn Weber is Head of Production Planning Systems in the Unternehmensgruppe Theo Müller and in this role, is responsible for the SAP modules PP and PP-PI there. He has detailed technical knowledge in the areas of process analysis, lean management, and production and capacity requirements planning. In his function, he supports the departments across Europe in the implementation of projects for setting up and optimizing new and existing business processes.

Previously he was employed a production planner at Röhm GmbH, one of the leading global manufacturers of clamping technology. As a project manager there, he was responsible for further development of the planning organization and processes in connection with SAP ERP and the detailed planning software wayRTS.

As an author, it is particularly important to Björn to convey his expertise as practically as possible and in a way that is easy to understand, and to attract the reader with the possibilities offered for further development in a company by using SAP for example, particularly in times of changing markets. Privately, Björn enjoys political and contemporary literature and his great hobby, photography.

Björn recently started a blog: *www.production-planning.blog*. In the blog he publishes short articles on the basic principles of production planning with the aim of passing on his knowledge to anyone starting out in this area. The blog also contains contributions on current trends in this field.

C Index

D Disclaimer

This publication contains references to the products of SAP SE.

SAP, R/3, SAP NetWeaver, Duet, PartnerEdge, ByDesign, SAP Busi-nessObjects Explorer, StreamWork, and other SAP products and ser-vices mentioned herein as well as their respective logos are trademarks or registered trademarks of SAP SE in Germany and other countries.

Business Objects and the Business Objects logo, BusinessObjects, Crystal Reports, Crystal Decisions, Web Intelligence, Xcelsius, and other Business Objects products and services mentioned herein as well as their respective logos are trademarks or registered trademarks of Busi-ness Objects Software Ltd. Business Objects is an SAP company.

Sybase and Adaptive Server, iAnywhere, Sybase 365, SQL Anywhere, and other Sybase products and services mentioned herein as well as their respective logos are trademarks or registered trademarks of Sybase, Inc. Sybase is an SAP company.

SAP SE is neither the author nor the publisher of this publication and is not responsible for its content. SAP Group shall not be liable for errors or omissions with respect to the materials. The only warranties for SAP Group products and services are those that are set forth in the express warranty statements accompanying such products and services, if any. Nothing herein should be construed as constituting an additional warr-anty.

More Espresso Tutorials Books

Tanya Duncan:

Practical Guide to SAP® CO-PC (Product Cost Controlling)

▶ Cost Center Planning Process and Costing Run Execution

▶ Actual Cost Analysis & Reporting

▶ Controlling Master Data

▶ Month End Processes in Details

http://5064.espresso-tutorials.com

Uwe Göhring:

Capacity Planning with SAP®

▶ How to leverage SAP Capacity Management

▶ Capacity planning best practices

▶ Options for capacity scheduling in SAP ERP

▶ Automatic resource and material scheduling with SAP APO

http://5080.espresso-tutorials.com

Avijt Dutta & Shreekant Shiralkar:

Demand Planning with SAP® APO— Concepts and Design

▶ Step-by-Step Explanations and Easy to Follow Instructions

▶ Combination of Theory, Business Relevance and 'How to' Approach

▶ APO DP Concepts and Design Explained using a Business Scenario

▶ Centralized Process Flow Diagram to Illustrate Integration

http://5105.espresso-tutorials.com

Avijt Dutta & Shreekant Shiralkar:

Demand Planning with SAP® APO— Execution

▶ Step-by-Step Explanations and Easy to Follow Instructions

▶ Combination of Theory, Business Relevance and 'How to' Approach

▶ APO DP Execution Explained using a Business Scenario

▶ Centralized Process Flow Diagram to Illustrate Integration

http://5106.espresso-tutorials.com

Rosana Fonseca:

Practical Guide to SAP® Material Ledger (ML)

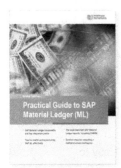

▶ SAP Material Ledger functionality and key integration points

▶ Tips for implementing and using SAP ML effectively

▶ The most important SAP Material Ledger reports, including CKM3N

▶ Detailed steps for executing a multilevel actual costing run

http://5116.espresso-tutorials.com

Tobias Götz, Anette Götz:

Practical Guide to SAP® Transportation Management (2nd edition)

▶ Supported business processes

▶ Best practices

▶ Integration aspects and architecture

▶ Comparison and differentiation to similar SAP components

http://5082.espresso-tutorials.com

Claudia Jost:

First Steps in the SAP® Purchasing Processes (MM), Second Edition

► Step-by-step instructions for creating a vendor master record and a purchase requisition

► How to convert a purchase requisition to a purchase order

► Approval process and credit approval procedure fundamentals

► Tips on how to create favorites

http://5166.espresso-tutorials.com/

Matthew Johnson:

SAP® Material Master—A Practical Guide, 2nd extended version

► Fundamental SAP Material Master concepts

► How settings impact other modules in SAP

► Cost-effective procurement and planning techniques

► Inventory and quality management best practices

http://5190.espresso-tutorials.com

www.ingramcontent.com/pod-product-compliance
Lightning Source LLC
Chambersburg PA
CBHW071142050326
40690CB00008B/1538